THE WORLD'S WEIRDEST WEB PAGES

AND THE PEOPLE WHO CREATE THEM

To a fellow appreciation of the "weirder" side of things!

hank duderstadt

no starch press

san francisco

**THE WORLD'S WEIRDEST WEB PAGES
AND THE PEOPLE WHO CREATE THEM**
©1996 by Hank Duderstadt

Printed in the United States of America

1 2 3 4 5 6 7 8 9 10—00 99 98 97 96

Trademarks
Trademarked names are used throughout this book. Rather than use a trademark symbol with every occurrence of a trademarked name, we are using the names only in an editorial fashion and to the benefit of the trademark owner, with no intention of infringement of the trademark.

Publisher: William Pollock
Cover and Interior Design: Derek Yee, Meredith Chew, Stacie Yamaki
Compositor: Derek Yee
Production and Development: Karol Jurado
Production Assistance: Carol Lombardi
Copyediting: Carol Lombardi
Proofreading: Michele Jones

Distributed to the book trade in the United States and Canada by
Publishers Group West, 4065 Hollis, P.O. Box 8843, Emeryville, California 94662
Phone: 800-788-3123 or 510-548-4393, Fax: 510-658-1834

For information on translations or book distributors outside the United States, please contact No Starch Press directly:
No Starch Press
401 China Basin Street, Suite 108, San Francisco, CA 94107-2192
phone: 415-284-9900; fax: 415-284-9955; info@nostarch.com; www.nostarch.com

Library of Congress Cataloging-in-Publication Data
Duderstadt, Mack (Mack Henry), 1958–
        The world's weirdest Web pages and the people who create them /
    Hank Duderstadt.
        p.   cm.
        ISBN 1-886411-12-3 (pbk.)
        1. World Wide Web (Information retrieval system)--Directories.
    2. Interviews.   I. Title.
    ZA4226.D84 1996
    025.04--dc20   96-32857
                                                           CIP

DEDICATION: *This book is dedicated to my dad, who helped instill a little "weirdness" into me at a very early age, telling me home-made fairy tales about characters like a little boy named Fatso Foogerty, who used to bring his lunch to school in two grocery bags. One day he got sick to his stomach, and...well...let's just say they had to call in the fire department to clean up...*

table of

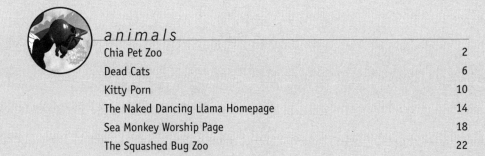

animals

contents

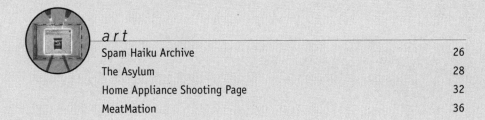

art

body parts

collections

food

introduction

I'LL NEVER FORGET MY FIRST ENCOUNTER WITH

THE WEB:

It was 1992, and the only advantage you got was being able to cruise boring text documents with the arrow keys on your keyboard. Select one, and whoops! You jumped to that page. It was a major league snooze.

Then I spent three days struggling with MacTCP. I finally got it running, connected to the Net, and launched Mosaic. The first page that laboriously drew onto my screen was NCSA, the creators of the program, but from there I quickly began to jump around. Sun Microsystems, Apple, Microsoft (boy, was it ugly then!), bianca's Smut Shack…BIANCA'S SMUT SHACK?!?!?! Yes, the third place I visited was The Shack—and immediately, I realized: Ethel, this is definitely not your traditional computer network.

After that, I discovered more weirdness than I had ever thought possible. Even then I understood that here was a place where anybody with a good (or bad, for that matter) idea, a little time, and access to a Web server could hang up their shingle. The result was that the Web, besides being an incredible source of information, was also a unique place to find entertainment. Those first few weird and wonderful sites have since grown into thousands, covering a truly vast array of perver—uh, topics.

Have you ever wondered what happens when you tape a strawberry Pop Tart into a toaster oven so that it can't eject, then start it? Or had this strange desire to build a religion based on your pet gerbil? Or take on Ann Landers and provide truly awful advice? In other words, have you ever had some deep-seated and seriously twisted desire that you've always fantasized about doing in public—kind of a virtual shedding your clothes and running through the Vatican during high mass on Christmas morning? Well if you have, then you're the perfect candidate to build your own twisted site—and this book will be great inspiration. If not, but you wonder what kind of sorry souls would get their jollies by placing a Twinkie in a microwave for ten minutes, then telling the world about what happens, this book is also for you.

So join me as we journey to the other side of cybertown, to the wrong side of the virtual railroad tracks. Hey, you don't need vaccinations or a bulletproof vest—just a sense of humor and an open mind.

animals

chia pet
zo

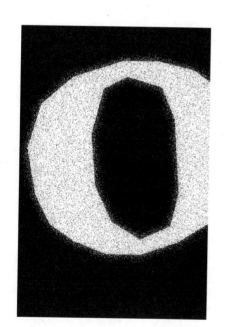

I've always had a kind of unusual love of kitsch. From the days of my youth, when I longed for a Pocket Fisherman or tasty julienne fries from a Veg-o-matic (my mother still has hers!) til more recently, when I've thought about getting some of the GH-12 (GH stands for Great Hair)—that stuff you spray on your head to disguise thinning hair—and then a Suck-n-Vac to keep it in check.

Still, they all pale in comparison to Chia Pets. It's a pet, it's a plant? These wonderful desk accessories with an identity crisis have always intrigued me. The only problem is that, after a while, the thought of having a furry lamb or even a Chia head gets kind of boring.

That's where the Chia Pet Zoo comes to the rescue with cyber-inspirations for all kinds of Chia wonders.

On it goes, relentlessly transforming people, places, and products into those wonderful plants.

WWW: What drove you to create this site?
JC: Initially I just wanted to see what creating a Web site was all about. But I had no real idea what to do with it. A friend happened to be in Yahoo! one day and found a site dedicated to Sea Monkeys, which inspired me to do the same for Chia Pets.

WWW: Were there any accomplices?
JC: Most of the inspiration and perspiration was mine, though I have a few folks who contribute graphics and ideas.

WWW: What are your goals?
JC: To continue to baffle people as to why anyone would waste their time doing such a zany, bizarre Web site.

WWW: How much effort was this page?
JC: The initial hurdle was learning HTML (which wasn't too tough) and teaching myself a few graphics editing tools. Now it doesn't take more than a few hours a week. Except when a new idea pops into my head, which means I gotta scramble for new graphics or whatever.

WWW: Where and how do you gather your content?
JC: Everywhere. Some is gleaned from dim corners of the Web; some comes from a digital camera I take when I drive around the Western states in the Blues Van.

WWW: What kind of reaction did your friends have to this site?
JC: "You did what? Why?" And a number of other reactions like that.

WWW: Your relatives?
JC: "Oh my, is this thing out in public?"

WWW: The local police?
JC: I kept a very low profile with our revered local law-enforcement personnel.

WWW: How has the Web-wandering community reacted to it?
JC: The Web site has inspired several folks to get off their butts and create their own site (some of which are kinda kool). Some express amazement at the variety of offerings on my page. Some actually ask if they can order Chia Pets! There are a number of requests for their own electronic pets, some of which I fulfill. I've gotten a few flame mails, but they're easily ignored.

WWW: How do you feel now that it's up?
JC: It's a GAS! I'd put a lot more effort into it if I wasn't distracted by my bloody job!

WWW: What's next?
JC: I'm working on more imaging techniques and some Java applets to enhance the site.

WWW: Have you learned any lessons from doing something this bizarre?
JC: Prepare yourself for the bizarre folks you attract.

WWW: What advice can you give other Web authors?
JC: Don't hesitate to go as far out as your truly bizarre imagination can take you. And further. That seems to be what piques the interest of others on the World Weird Web.

WWW: What kind of person would you like to attract to a site like this?
JC: Anyone interested in an imaginative, constantly changing, sometimes controversial, always bizarre site. Also anyone who gives me feedback.

Dead Cats

http://oucsace.cs.ohiou.edu/personal/apogue/dead.html

It's the 90s, and people are busy: busy trying to be more productive at work, busy trying to beat that biological clock and have a family, busy surfing the Web. In all this rush, the traditional pet may be just too much to handle. Add to this the fact that landlords are getting pickier every day.

The solution for those who still want animal companionship? How about a dead cat!

It's the perfect pet, your child's best friend, and a dust mop all in one. It doesn't eat, it doesn't make messes, and it doesn't explode in the microwave! What more could you ask for?

What more, indeed?! Just click to get your own Dead Cat Owner's Kit. Of course, this idea may be rather unsettling to cat lovers and other animal rights wack—er, advocates. If you're a tad touchy, you can "Ease your way into a new Dead Cat." As the copy soothes:

Dead Cat is made from all natural, 100% enviro-friendly materials. No poisonous or pollutive gases are emitted when ignited, roasted, boiled, broiled, baked, or nuked. Your Dead Cat is child-tolerant. In the rare event of a removed eye ball or severed limb, simply return your Dead Cat to our Dead Cat Vet for free repair.

For those who would like a more customized pet, a range of Specialty Dead Cats is offered, including Dead Cat on a Stick, The Bosnian Dead Cat (good as a mine detector), and of course Socks the Dead Cats (two to keep both your feet warm).

Of course, after you've gone to the trouble of getting your own dead cat, you may wonder, Now what? Check out some innovative suggestions on fun with fried felines:

3. Hang it by its tail for a Christmas tree ornament.

28. Dip it in water to moisten stamps.

29. Fill it with water, place it in the freezer overnight, and take it to work in your cooler.

32. Teach it to play dead.

68. Whack your stupid dog with them as a training aid.

71. With motion sensors, some short bungees tied to the roof, rat traps as launchers, and screaming cat sound effects, Dead Cats are 72% more effective at scaring off intruders than live dogs, guns, or Barry Manilow music.

Dead Cats may just be the answer for many of us who, in these rushed days, would like a little companionship but don't have the time to take care of a living pet. So, what next? Well, I once heard a story about a woman back East who had her husband stuffed after he'd passed away. Kept him in her sitting room for years.

by **ANGELA POGUE**

This was my father's brilliant idea. He told me that if pet rocks could be a profitable business, then dead cats would do even better. At the time, I was perhaps ten years old and very much opposed to any idea of selling dead cats. It was only a joke, but I took him quite seriously. He teased me about it, adding more and more details: He talked about how he would get the cats from a humane society so that there would be virtually no cost and then heighten the controversy and use the fuss as free advertising.

The teasing lasted only a day or two, but forever stuck vividly in my mind. I stumbled over the thought about a year back when joking with a friend. I told him the story, and within minutes we were both in tears laughing about the possibilities.

At the height of our laughter and absurdity, my friend says, "You should do a Dead Cat home page!" And so later that day, I did the first preliminary page and published it.

Over the following weeks, I would forward the e-mail responses to my friend with an attached comment or two, poking a bit of fun at what the people wrote. He then suggested that I publish the letters along with my comments—hence the Fan Mail Page.

The initial reaction was extreme in both directions. Either people felt the same as I did when I was ten, or as I do now. Of course there were the select few who responded with obscene comments. Once, someone went to the trouble to send me a detailed photo of dead cats at a humane society, and asked me to publish it. The picture was terribly disgusting and in no way humorous. It is safe to say I quickly deleted the .GIF.

As for my family, none of them know about the page, except my father. I showed it to him on a visit home in an attempt to get him interested in the Internet. He didn't get it, which was a bit of a disappointment. I'm quite sure he has forgotten about it by now. Friends within my present and past universities quickly stumbled upon it. A few told me that I must have serious mental problems (chuckling under their breath all the while). Jokes are made here and there, followed by with acute leeriness around me. I enjoy it.

Lessons I've learned? This is publishing. People like aesthetic quality with original content that keeps their attention. They also like interaction with immediate feedback both in responses via e-mail and in page updates. It's a lot to handle sometimes and takes a bit of commitment, but when I have the time to bother, I have a ball playing with it.

The only advice I can offer someone desiring to publish their own page is to get some Web space, an e-mail address, an HTML reference manual, and go at it. There are of course tricks of the trade like registering your page and so on, but all that is secondary to the page itself. Just keep in mind that it's all in good fun, and any limitations are self-imposed.

Kitty

In a recent study conducted by Richard Little it is estimated that there are over a million billion pictures of cats on the Internet. That number is expected to rise by some 30,000,000% over the next year. Projections for the year 2010 show that there will be more cat pictures on the Internet than molecules of oxygen in the atmosphere.

Of course, it's admitted that Richard is only 10-years old—but he's the only one doing research on this important issue.

What is the evil force behind this cat abuse? References are made to a shadowy group called the Feline Mafia Organization (or FMO)—and even the federal government has become involved. A picture of Socks, the Clintons' cat, has been posted by the Smithsonian. Even syndicated columnist Puddy, of "Ask Puddy" fame, has remained remarkably silent about this sad reality.

Is there any hope for all those helpless kittens?

The Coalition of Those Attempting to Think Clearly and Probably Failing provides one possible solution:

Society should spend a lot more time trying to educate and help people stay mentally and physically healthy instead of making them sick and then trying to stop them from hurting each other. If we must pass laws about pornography on the Internet, we advise a law that requires EVERYONE on the Internet to post a pornographic picture of themselves. We don't know if that would solve the problem, but it would sure be interesting.

10

The Internet has often been compared to the Wild West: a lawless place where anarchy reigns, criminals wander freely, and sex is cheap and easy to get—or at least grainy pictures of it! Yet, when the supporters of the Communications Decency Act spoke out in an attempt to bring "law and order" to the Information Super —Hypeway, they failed to point out one of the most heinous and disturbing types of pornography transmitted online. Or so the members of THE CORPORATION write:

A young man using the handle "flea" uploads a pornographic picture to an Internet newsgroup. It happens an estimated 2,000 times a day, but this time, it's different. The picture shows a naked six year old, who we will call Kathy, helplessly tied in thin blue yarn—and what is perhaps even more disturbing, the man distributing the picture is Kathy's legal guardian. To this date, no legal action has been taken and Kathy is still in the custody of "flea." Why has justice failed Kathy? Why has the law not intervened?

The answer is simple—Kathy is a cat.

Kitty Porn is a Web site with a mission to protect those that cannot protect themselves—at least unless they get really ticked off and go after you with their claws.

The page informs us that dozens of pictures of hapless felines are posted on the Net every day without their permission.

11

WWW: What was your inspiration for this site?

RB: An incipient collective nervous breakdown and an overdose of unfunny top-ten lists. Actually, sifting through the millions of sites on the Internet that didn't particularly speak to us made us realize that our voice wasn't out there yet, and probably wouldn't be, unless we spoke up. Even with the vast number of sites on the Internet, you can do something original if you are being true to yourself. The fact that there are a lot of possibilities that haven't been explored yet on the Web is good inspiration for anyone to do that project or tell that story they've always wanted to. Millions of people are out there waiting for decent content

WWW: Were there any accomplices?

RB: Presently sitting on The Board of THE CORPORATION are Paul Pierce, Reed Berkowitz, and Tim Pennington-Russell. It is a joint venture of Hostile Takeover and Cybernautics of Sausalito, California.

WWW: What are your goals?

RB: Our goal is to provide peace and laughter to a cold, heartless world. Probably this one.

WWW: How much effort was this page?

RB: Thousands of employees in 23 countries contribute to the production of THE CORPORATION's humor product. Most of them haven't been paid and have been on strike for about 3½ years. So Paul, Reed and Tim are forced to do most of the work.

WWW: Where and how do you gather your content?
RB: Our best material comes from undergoing hypnosis. Horrific childhood memories surface and are then twisted into finely crafted pieces of humor product. Occasionally we fast. If all else fails, we just think up funny and relevant material and make some pages out of it.

WWW: What kind of reaction did your friends have to this site?
RB: They said, "But you're not funny. You've never been funny. It's like a blind person piloting a large aircraft. What can you possibly be thinking? You should really get into real estate."

WWW: Your relatives?
RB: They asked, "What is the World Wide Web?" to which we replied, "It's like a boring slide show, only the pictures don't appear right away and the text is small and almost unreadable," to which they replied, "Could you pass the turnips?"

WWW: The local police?
RB: THE CORPORATION controls most urban law enforcement organizations. Our men and women in blue are required to laugh and be generally jovial when asked about THE CORPORATION.

WWW: How has the Web-wandering community reacted to it?
RB: Favorably. We've gotten some nice fan mail and have received some nice awards for our efforts.

WWW: How do you feel now that it's up?
RB: Compelled to make the site bigger and better. When you know that tons of people are going to look at what you've done, you try to make it as good as it can possibly be, given time and money constraints.

WWW: What's next?
RB: We are currently hard at work on THE CORPORATION bible, which will soon be available from quality religions everywhere. After that, we really need to take out the garbage and do the dishes. And the laundry.

WWW: Have you learned any lessons from doing something this bizarre?
RB: Definitely. That humankind is doomed to a violent and painful demise. And that bananas are quite possibly the world's most perfect food.

WWW: What words of wisdom can you give others who want to publish on the Web?
RB: DO IT! Please just do it. This is the classic beauty of the WWW: It's the world's largest Show and Tell. If you have something to say, no matter how strange (or boring, even) say it! We're still at a point where individuals can produce great sites and get some recognition. Don't be intimidated. If anybody gives you any trouble, just tell them THE CORPORATION said to "BACK OFF!"

WWW: What kind of person would you like to attract to a site like this?
RB: Our actuarial studies show that we tend to attract mostly African-American women over the age of 60. However, we'd like to attract anyone with a sense of humor. And a lot of loose, fast money.

THE NAKED DANCING LLAMA HOMEPAGE

Are you frustrated with the sparse range of choices you have in the upcoming presidential election? Even if you disregard the nominees of the Republications or Demoncrats, the others really don't leave much hope, either. I have seen the answer, and like so many great things these days, it lives on the World Wide Web!

The Naked Dancing Llama (NDL) Page states "I'm running for President because America must remember how to frolic like a llama before it is too late." The Naked Dancing Llama itself (to be honest, I'm still not sure whether it's a he or a she) is an advice-giving, frolicking, tangoing, peanut-spitting llama who is here to help you with your problems! Some of the typical advice that NDL has given in the past follows:

Dear NDL,
*What would motivate a
seemingly rational
person to take a shower
while not fully naked?
Signed, Showering*

**Dear Showering,
I don't have that problem.
I'm always naked.
NDL**

*Dear Naked Dancing Llama,
As a llama, is it as much fun
to squish Spam between your
toes as it is for a human? Also,
if you could be any kind of
algae, what kind would you be?
Signed, Very Curious*

**Dear Very Curious,
1. I don't have toes, I have
HOOVES.**

**2. I have long pondered what
kind of algae I would like to
be. I would like to be a big
algae. Big. Like Lake Erie.
Sincerely, NDL**

Does this hoofed candi-
date really pose a threat
to the likes of Bob Dole
and Bill Clinton? That remains to be seen. But,
from what I understand,
the NDL has been seen
frolicking with H. Ross
Perot, and the voting's
not over yet.

WWW: What was your inspiration for this site?

CF: I created the Naked Dancing Llama site in response to big business coming to the Internet. I'm a Web page designer at the University of Wisconsin, White-water. I had become too used to seeing normal pages on the Web.

In addition, there is a real story to the creation of NDL. I visit a talker called the Vineyard (vineyard.igc.net 4242), and they were in the process of deleting bad words as user names. The only way to delete these names was to login using the bad words. So I came in as bad word after bad word. Eventually, I had to get creative. But those running the chat realized I was having too much fun being booted off, so when I came on as

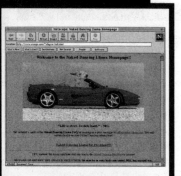

Naked Dancing Llama, they let me stay.

WWW: Were there any accomplices?

CF: Yes. A friend, Nathan Soderland, and many others helped develop NDL. I brought him to the Web, and decided to have him be an advice-giving llama.

WWW: What are your goals?

CF: My goals are:

1. Get NDL to be President of the United States.

2. Give great advice, and help cheer up people on the Web who are surfing— looking for something that is actually funny.

3. Provide a site un-like any other on the Internet that will get no dupli-cate matches from a search engine.

4. Dance, dance, dance like a llama would dance.

WWW: How much effort was this page?
CF: At first, this page was only minimal effort. But again, that's because no one knew about it. After Yahoo! gave it Site of the Week, and I got published in the *Milwaukee Journal Sentinel*, it became more of a chore to maintain. And it hit me right near exam week, so I had some disgruntled llama supporters wondering why I hadn't responded to their e-mails. Now, it's pretty much updated three times a month with campaign information, llama advice, and the occasional flying aardvark.

WWW: Where and how do you gather your content?
CF: Llama mail contributes a lot of my content. I also check Usenet, go to talkers as NDL, and whenever I need a graphic I run to Alta Vista.

WWW: What kind of reaction did your friends have to this site?
CF: My friends were completely indifferent about this site. You see, at Whitewater, they all were developing home pages for the different departments on campus, and my site, was, well, weird, and required a bit of imagination to comprehend. But suddenly they lightened up when they realized I was getting a lot of hits. Typical really.

WWW: Your relatives?
CF: My relatives are REALLY supportive of me on the Net. Helping to distribute and mail Naked Dancing Llama T-shirts, getting me a dedicated connection to the Internet. Not that any of them understand the Internet yet. :)

WWW: The local police?
CF: The local police have been nice to NDL and have not arrested me yet for having a llama in my basement.

WWW: How has the Web-wandering community reacted to it?
CF: Well, various reactions. Some e-mails say I am a genius, others say I just have too much time on my hands, others say how they are falling in love with a naked dancing llama. I love the Net.

WWW: How do you feel now that it's up?
CF: That's a very personal question.

WWW: What next?
CF: Next comes the NDL fan club—FONDL (Friend of Naked Dancing Llama)—then, who knows? After I graduate I hope to work for *Wired* or another such magazine.

WWW: Have you learned any lessons from doing something this bizarre?
CF: Yes. There are a LOT of weird people out there. It's a relief.

WWW: What words of wisdom can you give others who want to publish on the Web?
CF: DO IT. And say exactly what you want to say and mean it. And make it look nice and people might actually take you seriously.

WWW: What kind of person would you like to attract to a site like this?
CF: What kind of person? ANYONE who is looking for something new and different on the Web, needs a good laugh, or wants something strange on their screen to help them keep perspective as they tap away at an Excel spreadsheet.

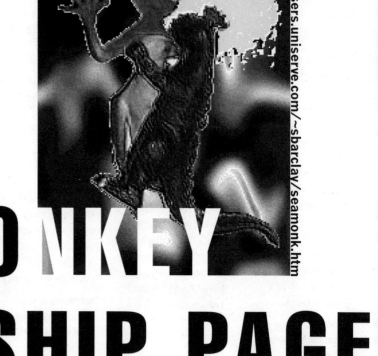

http://users.uniserve.com/~sbarclay/seamonk.htm

SEA MONKEY
WORSHIP PAGE

Remember newspapers like GRIT? I could have cared less about the features—I'd just jump to the back, where they had lots of neat stuff for sale: seeds to satisfy the most aggressive gardener; porcelain figurines that were so cute they made your teeth hurt; gadgets galore to do everything from slicing up your veggies to feeding Rover.

Then there were Sea Monkeys. Just looking at the ad would make any self-respecting kid dream of having one of these nautical families living in a bowl on their bookcase. Imagine all the hours of fun watching them play and frolic. The fact that they were still raring to go, even though it took *six to eight weeks* for them to show up, should have been a warning. Or that they came in a foil packet that looked more like chili seasoning than a haven for fun pets. But thousands of American kids did, still do, and probably always will invite these critters into their lives. No wonder, then, that there's a Sea Monkey Worship Page with more information about these wonders of the deep than you thought possible. Included are tips on how (and how NOT) to raise your family of fun:

Don't lie—Sea Monkeys don't like it when people lie to them any more than people do.

Don't give them bananas—they may be monkeys, but they will be suffocated by the large banana in their little tank.

Don't scream "Hey, look at the Sea Monkeys" at them—they don't like to be reminded of their existence. (Sea Monkeys are docile creatures who prefer to remain clear of existential thought.) Similarly, Buddhist koans such as "What is the sound of one hand clapping?" might make the Sea Monkeys realize the meaningless of their existence and this could cause mass Sea Monkey suicide.

Do cover the Sea Monkey tank while engaged in marital relations, because Sea Monkeys carry camcorders and aren't afraid to sell those tapes to Hard Copy.

There's an interview with Sea Monkey creator Harol Von Braunhut. There's a Sea Monkey Christmas Page, A Sea Monkey Birth Announcements Page, a Wall O' Grief for people whose Sea Monkeys passed away, and even a Sea Monkey Obsessional Quiz, which includes questions like:

1. Do you dream about Sea Monkeys? (Give yourself an extra point if these are particularly naughty dreams).

2. Have you given each Sea Monkey a name and can you identify each Monkey by sight? (An extra point if you have figured out each Monkey's individual personality).

3. Do you scour the toy stores and comic books for extra Sea Monkey accessories?

4. Have you ever awakened in the morning with an "Amazing Live Sea-Monkey's SEA-BUBBLE™" around your neck and didn't know where it came from?

So for the Sea Monkey lover, the Sea Monkey Worship Page is truly the end-all be-all. Of course, if you're like me and long ago realized that these things are actually brine shrimp in disguise—well, there's always the Chia Pet Zoo (see page 2).

interview with **SUSAN BARCLAY**

WWW: What was your inspiration for this site?
SB: My inspirations were threefold:

1. My ISP provides free Web-page creation and storage;

2. I wanted to see my name on the Web; and

3. I am obsessed with Sea Monkeys and want to share my rantings with others.

My friends think that I will do anything for a laugh, including maiming someone, so this was the ideal situation to put my bizarre ideas into print. One of the first things I searched for when I obtained Web access in February '95 was a site for Sea Monkeys and, much to my surprise, I did not find one. Thus the worship page was born.

WWW: Were there any accomplices?
SB: My boyfriend, Raymond Nichols, helped with the creation of the initial page and the list of "do's and don'ts" for Sea Monkey survival. My mom, dad, and friends Wanda Smith and Michelle Prokop have made numerous suggestions for interesting additions.

WWW: What are your goals?
SB: My goals are world domination by Sea Monkey enthusiasts and the creation of a page that might make people laugh just once during the day. Sea Monkeys are a metaphor for an ideal human world: non-cannibalistic, peaceful, communal, and disposable. If all of our leaders were Sea Monkeys, there would be no wars, no poverty, no child abuse, and no rude hand gestures in

traffic. Secondly, I hope that people reading my page will be inspired to write questions or share their poetry with me. I try to include everything I can find about Sea Monkeys, from sonnets to cross-stitch patterns to comic strips.

WWW: How much effort was this page?
SB: This page was initially very easy to maintain. The questions, answers, and poetry came from my deranged imagination. Once people became interested in the page, they began sending me a great deal of mail. I strive to answer all of it. This now takes approximately 20 hours per month—two days of power reading, typing, and FTP'ing info to the ISP.

WWW: Where and how do you gather your content?
SB: Most of the information is submitted by Sea Monkey enthusiasts who send birth announcements, grief notices, poems, or questions. In addition, I use a lot of information from the Sea Monkey catalogue, because it has some (unintentionally) funny writing in it.

WWW: What kind of reaction did your friends have to this site?
SB: Most of my friends have been very supportive and advertise my site on their sites or in their e-mail signatures! The odd friend has expressed concerns about my mental fitness but, other than those mindless idiots, I have had nothing but praise (and large cash donations). I am aware of one who called the local mental health

authority, which led to a battery of tests about voices in my head, but I was released in the required 72 hours and continue to work on this page unhindered.

WWW: Your relatives?
SB: My dad is right into the page and regularly asks me about the messages I receive. He is still trying to find a way to make some money from this venture, but I refuse to make the Net commercial (actually, I can't come up with a way to make money either, but I use the other excuse more often). My mother merely shakes her head and rues the day that she turned down my Ritalin prescription. My relatives in England have seen the page and appear to be interested, but I think most of them are glad that I am adopted and the gene pool remains unblemished!

WWW: The local police?
SB: The RCMP are aware of me and, come to think of it, I *have* noticed an increase in their drive-by patrols lately. Oh great, now you've made me paranoid—which is not a great addition to my obsessive/compulsive nature!

WWW: How has the Web-wandering community reacted to it?
SB: I have received a great response to my page, including various awards such as the Weird on the Web award and Burning Bacon with Bartlett [sic]. I receive lots of e-mail every day, most of it is positive and well thought out!

WWW: How do you feel now that it's up?
SB: Fantastic. Most mornings I awake to another e-mail message heaping praise on me. That is one heck of a way to start my day—as opposed to finding a mutilated alarm clock on the floor!

WWW: What's next?
SB: I have two ideas for further Web pages—the first being about a new product similar to Sea Monkeys that the good people at Transcience are putting out (all very top secret), and the second being a tribute to the little plastic bird in a top hat who bobs up and down in a glass of water. My current plans are to keep updating the page and to continue my quest for world domination.

WWW: Have you learned any lessons from doing something this bizarre?
SB: That people are weird. Not everyone, mind you, but most. Under the "normal" exterior of your friends and family members lies a group of crazy people who want to be weird for just a while! In addition, I've become very aware for the need for free speech on the Net (insert debate here) and the value of access to anyone with an idea and an ISP who wants to become their own publisher!

WWW: What advice do you have for others who want to publish on the Web?
SB: Just do it (uh oh, copyright infringement—I'll have to think of another). I would recommend that they put their ideas on a site and see what results. If your work is interesting, funny, controversial, awe inspiring or just weird, it belongs on the Web so others can take a look at it and enjoy what lurks in your mind! Ensure that you can convey your message properly—i.e., use a spellchecker—and do it in a fresh and interesting way. Don't be scared—someone out there is bound to enjoy your rantings.

WWW: What kind of person would you like to attract to a site like this?
SB: My motto (if I had one) is: Come one, come all, come see the freak that is the Sea Monkey Worship Page. Anyone who wants to know more about Sea Monkeys is welcome to my site!

the squashed bugzoo

http://squashed.roach.org/zoo.html

Did you hear the one about how to tell if bikers are happy? Count the bugs on their teeth. All right, everyone, let's hear it:

Eeeeewwweeeewwwwwwwww!!

If you think that's disgusting, then prepare yourself for a Web site that salutes those insects who suffered the number-one cause of death among their kind: getting squashed.

The Squashed Bug Zoo isn't necessarily disgusting in the same sort of gross-out, gooey, better-find-a-spare-airsick-bag kind of way that some pages are (for that, you'd better point your browser at the SpamCam, page 82).

But it's still pretty unappetizing.

Here you'll find ravaged roaches, squished silverfish, brutalized beetles, and all kinds of crushed creepy-crawlies. In addition to various insects, the zoo even has a section for other animals, including (at the time of my first visit) a mouse, a rat, and something that nobody could seem to figure out.

If the bashed bugs aren't enough for you, then you can jump over to the Comments page to read more about these little critters and get details about their untimely demises.

Even in their rathered flattened, immobile state, these smallest of God's creatures have provided a kind of twisted entertainment for the more bizarre of us.

22

interview with **MATTHEW J. COLLINS**

WWW: What was your inspiration for this site?
MC: Bugs. The bugs made me do it. They hate me. I hate them. Bugs. Bugs.

WWW: Were there any accomplices?
MC: Yes. Bad bugs who hate other bugs. And the roach.

WWW: What are your goals?
MC: Five to nothing versus the Wolverhampton Wanderers.

WWW: How much effort was this page?
MC: Not much, I just had to fill out a silly questionnaire, and the bugs did the rest.

WWW: Where and how do you gather your content?
MC: I let people send it to me. Very hard. Sometimes I get the bugs themselves through the mail instead of just pictures. Once I had a weird bug squashers-

fetishist type catalog and book sent to me. This all goes on the page whenever I can be bothered. Or when the bugs get angry.

WWW: What kind of reaction did your friends have to this site?
MC: They told me I was a bug.

WWW: Your relatives?
MC: They *are* bugs.

WWW: How has the Web-wandering community reacted to it?
MC: With bugspray. Oh, and accesses. And mailbombs.

WWW: How do you feel now that it's up?
MC: Like I did before.

WWW: What's next?
MC: World domination by Tuesday teatime.

WWW: Have you learned any lessons from doing something this bizarre?
MC: I get lots of silly questionnaires and interview requests.

WWW: What words of wisdom can you offer other Web publishers?
MC: Do it. The bugs will forgive you.

WWW: What kind of person would you like to attract to your site?
MC: Someone who isn't writing a book about it.

squashed bug zoo

art

The Web has become a whole new cultural medium: From the vast literary treasure that is the Library of Congress to the beautiful works of art in the Louvre, the Web is a haven for all kinds of culture lovers. Even really twisted ones.

Witness the SPAM Haiku Archive. Here, over 4,000 examples of "Spamku" are available for the more adventurous literary types. OK, I realize that my college English professors would probably gasp at some of these—but it's all art, right?

> *Ate three cans of SPAM,*
> *But there's still room for Jell-O.*
> *I love this country.*

> *A half-eaten slice.*
> *Ants swarm the cold, greasy plate.*
> *A suicide note.*

> *A SPAM loaf quivers.*
> *Salivary glands juice up.*
> *Anticipation.*

Besides Haiku, the SPAM Haiku Archive also features SPAM Limericks and SPAM Sonnets for the truly brave at heart.

John Nagamichi Cho has put a lot of effort into this collection. Though the visuals on his pages are a little sparse, the heart (and for that matter lung, liver, kidneys—I mean, this is SPAM we're talking about) is there.

SPAM HAIKU

http://www.naic.edu/~jcho/spam/sha.html

WWW: What was your inspiration for this site?
JNC: SPAM made me do it. I blame Jay Hormel.

WWW: Were there any accomplices?
JNC: Yes. Phil Erickson (pje@hyperion. haystack.edu) and Alec Proudfoot (alec@netcom.com). They provided inspiration and technical assistance.

WWW: What are your goals?
JNC: To have people not take things too seriously, and for them to get off their butts and write some creative things rather than just passively reading them on the Web.

WWW: How much effort was this page?
JNC: It probably takes a couple of hours every week to maintain.

WWW: Where and how do you gather your content?
JNC: "If you build it, they will come." That's exactly what happened. It's helped that the media has picked it up. I've been interviewed by the *New York Times*, *Chicago Tribune*, the BBC—even France's *Le Monde* wrote about the archive!

WWW: What kind of reaction did your friends have to this site?
JNC: Some have responded by contributing entries to the archive, others just thought this simply confirmed their belief that I was very weird.

WWW: Your relatives?
JNC: Not many know (because I don't keep in close touch with most relatives). Only a few of them get it.

WWW: How has the Web-wandering community reacted to it?
JNC: BIG response. I have about 600 con-tributors now, with over 4,300 entries in total. Plus lots of fan mail. Only a couple of negative e-mails since the archive opened in June 1995.

WWW: How do you feel now that it's up?
JNC: Like it's my fifteen minutes of fame.

WWW: What's next?
JNC: I've been trying to find a publisher for a Book of Spamku. So far they have been afraid of a Hormel lawsuit.

WWW: Have you learned any lessons from doing something this bizarre?
JNC: It's relatively easy to become popular on the Web. And journalists tend to copy each other.

WWW: What words of wisdom can you give others who want to publish on the Web?
JNC: JUST DO IT. HTML is very easy.

spam haiku archive

THE ASYLUM

Space Boy
(24 x 24)
by Kelly Larson on *July 13, 1995*

http://www.asylum.cid.com/

Since my very first journey out onto the World Wide Web, I always had a knack for finding the more unusual sites. One of the first of these "alternative" places in Cyberspace was the Asylum, an incredible collection of games and weirdness that still rivals anything out there.

Even in the early days of the Web, the inmates—er, creators of the Asylum weren't happy with cute graphics and humor text. They wanted to build multimedia. The first example I ever encountered online was their WWW LiteBoard, patterned after The Lite-Brite, that great toy many of us had as kids. Here you can actually try your hand at a virtual board, and if your work's impressive enough, it gets added to the gallery.

Another classic is the Cuckoo Clock. I'll never forget clicking on the icon and then waiting several minutes just to hear some totally twisted sound come out of my computer. Though this is pretty basic stuff in today's world of Shockwave and RealAudio, it's still funny.

WYSIWYG is the name given to the pet cockroach that lives at the Asylum. Give her a piece of Twinkie and you'll get a response like:

WYSIWYG thanks you for your kind deed. Except for the sludge underneath the refrigerator, Twinkies are her favorite food! For your act of kindness, your site has been placed on the Good Karma list, where it will be given the highest available access priority.

Another seriously cool area is the Fiction Therapy group, where you can contribute to a great work of literature under construction:

I was sitting in my office staring out the window watching the inmates across the street at The Asylum playing with their Lite-Brites. Suddenly, I heard a knock on the door.

Without me saying a word, the person behind the door saw fit to enter and alas, it was my tormentor. I grabbed my chainsaw from behind the desk just in case there was trouble. Sensing danger, he got the hell out of my office, but on his way out, a piece of paper fell from his jacket. I looked at the paper. It was covered with points. It smelled like that urine - ketchup - rosy sort of smell, you know the one.

Actually I don't know the one, but that's another story.

There she was, lying nude on the floor, once again. Thumbtacks were everywhere. There was a place on the floor without any thumbtacks; I leapt over and realized in the air that she was lying on that spot. But what could I do about that now? You're right. Nothing. Agility was never my strong point—I landed and I landed hard. (Yeah, she was a looker all right.) It was a dark and stormy night. I looked at her luxurious body once more. Hmmm, I thought: "This luxurious dead body must be a clue!" Then she licked me. That lick was kind of like the rough cloying lick of a cat, a big game cat.

Among the more recent additions is the Virtual Dartboard. You're given two targets (the time I went it was Barney and Godzilla) and custom designed of darts to choose, depending on whether you love or hate the target. Whatever you use is left there for all to see. Hmmmmm... Godzilla had more "kisses" and Barney had more "mushroom clouds."

The Asylum has enough to keep anyone busy for hours, but is it seriously twisted like, say, Dan's Gallery of the Grotesque (see page 120)? No— but then again, after all the therapy the inmates have had, I guess that figures.

WWW: What's the nativity myth for The Asylum?

J: It started as a competition to get hits. Aure and I had our own junk, getting hits, and then we decided we could put it all together into one big thing.

A: We got some hits; we had some fun; we got some crazy e-mails. We got a taste of the "fame" that is being on the Web and being popular.

WWW: What was on it when it started?

J: Lite-Board, Rev Door, Cuckoo Clock. Barney wasn't in there yet. WYSIWYG the mascot, Empty TV. The Mechanical Bull was there, which is just a free-for-all. Inmates, where you can post your nightmares; and the Poll, where you can vote and choose the most popular thing. This was the first poll where you could just click up and down and get your answers right away.

WWW: Do you remember how you came up with WYSIWYG?

A: I hate WYSIWYG.

J: We looked around, and other sites had mascots, so we had to have a mascot. The Void was the coolest site (http://kao.ini.cmu.edu:5550/). They had the Blue Dog, who can count. So Blue Dog was their mascot, WYSIWYG is our mascot.

WWW: When did the Asylum actually go up?

A: It was launched on the Ides of May, 1994.

WWW: How long did it take for you to get all your stuff together?

J: About two weeks, I guess.

WWW: Where did the name come from?

A: Joe had a list of stupid names he thought of, and one day I just thought of it, and I knew immediately that there was no other name. He wanted to call it "The Core Dump." We used that as a part of it, for the place where we put the stuff that just didn't quite make any sense anywhere else.

WWW: What were you doing when you thought of it?
A: We knew it was going to be a wacky place and we were trying to think of a cool thing and it just came. (*in hippie voice*) Muses, man.

WWW: What were your big influences?
J: The Web was starting to go around campus.

A: The big names were Andrew/WERDNA (Andrew Tong, now at http://cruciform.cid. com/~werdna/), Rei Thigpen at MIT. Andrew's page, for some reason, was hit like crazy. There's a certain mystique about CalTech students—you don't know which one is that megalosaurus character who's going to change the world. The first time I tried to contact Andrew about a script or something, he basically blew me off. Just gave me a real quick answer or maybe a URL to look at.

J: Then we begged him to link to us.

A: Yeah, right before the launch of The Asylum, we said: "OK, now we've got to advertise it—wouldn't it be great if we got it on Andrew's page?" Joe was probably even heard murmuring things like: "I just want to create a page that belittles WERDNA." So it was kind of that friendly competition.

WWW: What else gave birth to it?
J: Too much time surfing the Web, seeing what other people were doing and going, "Oh, that's kind of cute, but we can do a lot better."

WWW: The Ides of May. Was this right before exams?
J: No, I was doing research. I mean I was neglecting research.

WWW: What kind?
J: You know, thesis research. Shockwave focusing. Aeronautics. Rocket science. There you go. You just get that in there somewhere.

WWW: When did The Asylum move to http:// www.asylum.cid.com/?
A: Around the time that Joe got married, January 1996.

WWW: Was it a natural move? I mean, Creative Internet Design is about a year old now.
A: Yeah, we incorporated around June '95. But we're still at CalTech. We're still in Pasadena.

J: *You* are.

A: Oh right, like the ink's dry on your Ph.D.

WWW: So is the message that The Asylum was all a product of your warped imaginations while nothing interesting was going on in your lives?
A: Are you saying "aero" isn't interesting?

J: And now we hardly get any time to do new Asylum stuff because ...

A: Because I keep Joe working like a dog all the time doing the work we get *paid* for.

HOME AP

Question: How many times have you wanted to kill a machine—you know, take a sledgehammer to that VCR you never figured out how to program? Or use a .44 Magnum ("The world's most powerful handgun. It could blow your head clean off!") on the PC that keeps eating your floppies?

Dan Benton, for one, has put his words into actions, and he put the resulting photographs on the Web at the Home Appliance Shooting Page.

"Over the last decade, I've shot many, many electro-mechanical devices to pieces. This has included televisions, microwave ovens, and all sorts of other stuff that looked fun to shoot."

The H.A.S. has pulverized enough appliances to satisfy the most rabid Luddite:

SHOT

PLIANCE

An old console TV

A microwave oven

A reel-to-reel tape recorder

And on and on he goes, raining destruction down upon helpless appliances.

For some folks, visions of a serious Second Amendment junkie/gun nut might come into focus. I mean, this guy is into serious mayhem. But ask yourself: How many times have you dreamt of taking an AR-15 with a 50-round banana clip to that CD player that keeps skipping in the best part of your favorite album? Or a sawed–off 12-gauge shotgun with double-0 buckshot to that lawn mower that will only start after 15 pulls of the cord? Or a 12-megaton thermonuclear bomb to that bus that roared away from the stop just as you ran up to catch it—OK, OK, that might be going a bit far.

The next time the Ford's on the fritz, the microwave's mangled, or the computer's crashed, and you find yourself eyeing that spare hammer in your workshop with malice, don't get mad—surf over to Dan's Home Appliance Shooting Page.

ING PAGE

interview with **DAN BENTON**

WWW: What drove you to create this site?
DB: I'd seen a lot of "Me too!" sites, so I wanted to do something a little different. I looked for something in my life that few, if any, other people did.

WWW: Were there any accomplices?
DB: My three brothers—Mike, William, and James.

WWW: What are your goals?
DB: I actually wanted to have a little fun with the page. I didn't have any large goals, I just wanted to give people a good laugh. So far, it has made Mirsky's WOTW, was a Yahoo! Site of the Week, and also made a number of smaller site lists. I'd like to make Cool Site of the Day, but I'll wait for H.A.S. #2 to do this. It will be *Cool*. Maybe Geek Site of the Day.

WWW: How much effort did this page take?
DB: About a decade of shooting, and maybe 4–8 hours of computer work.

WWW: Where and how do you gather your content?
DB: I looked at a number of old photos, found the negatives, and had a Kodak PhotoCD made. I used OS/2 and the PhotoCD to make JPGs. I then took the JPGs to my Linux box and cropped them with the program XV.

WWW: What kind of reaction did your friends have to this site?
DB: They all saw the humor in this page and laughed about it. The employees at my new job like it. I was told by a number of people in the system administration group that I should be in

their group, not the Web design group, because they had seen my H.A.S. page. They said I'd fit right in.

WWW: Your relatives?
DB: They also see the humor here.

WWW: The local police?
DB: Don't know. I didn't break any law, so they don't matter.

WWW: How has the Web-wandering community reacted?
DB: Except for three losers who wouldn't leave their e-mail addresses and a single jerkoff from Tallahassee, Florida, all the reactions have been positive. I've gotten nearly a thousand messages over the last year. Many people send stories of their own "hunting" experiences.

WWW: How do you feel now that it's up?
DB: I'm happy with it. I wish I'd included sounds on the first cut.

WWW: What's next?
DB: Version 2 with sound, stills, and movies. A number of people at my new job (at Supernet, Inc.) want to come along a help out. I'm going to have 2–4 camcorders, 2–4 cameras, 5+ shotguns, handguns, rifles, monitors, TVs, terminals, VCRs, CD players, and all sorts of other junk to blast. It's gonna be a *BLAST*!

WWW: Have you learned any lessons from doing something this bizarre?
DB: Is it bizarre? It's just plinking with a twist.

WWW: What words of wisdom can you give other potential Web authors?
DB: Avoid Frames, Java, and hard-to-read font/color combinations. Maybe use Java in six months or so. Only use Frames if it's required, not just because you know how.

Try to make it look like either an index (that's what I did) or a printed page of text.

WWW: What sort of person would you like to attract to a site like this?
DB: Anyone who likes a good laugh.

MEATMATION

Stephanie Rose
loves to

PRICE PER LB.
6.99

DATE
05.29.9

http://www.cais.net/frisch/meatmation/

0.00

interview with **STEPHANIE ROSE**

WWW: Where did you find your inspiration?
SR: I was doing a lot of ceramics and sculpture for my major. I was trying to think of different mediums I could use one day. I

always thought that it'd be interesting to sculpt with ground beef. Ground beef has a texture kind of like clay, and I thought it would be interesting to play with meat. I

don't know, it sounded kind of funny to me. So I needed to do a project for my color photography class and I thought what's a better color than meat. I was origi-

NET WT LB.

TOTAL

No, I'm not talking about just moving her peas around, or even trying to build a miniature Mt. Everest out of mashed potatoes. I'm talking serious *play*. Like building a family of meat products—MeatMation—definitely not a Web site for vegetarians.

MeatMation follows the continuing adventures of Mr. Beefy and his Beefeater family—a family made of meat. Stephanie's original concept was that Mr. Beefy would realize that his whole family was edible and would eat them one by one, until he was left alone—still hungry but unscathed. Turns out his legs are made of chicken.

As you wander through the story of the Beefeater clan you'll find hyperlinks to other food-related sites, like "fish" links to a recipe for shrimp alfredo and "carrots" which bring you to a recipe for Chilled Carrot Herb Soup Manquit. These links are cute, but the real fun is in the seriously sick story. The Beefeater family starts out hungry and so Pa goes fishin'. Problem is that Grandma is made of fish and before you know it, she's been caught ... and eaten. From there, the plot gets ever more twisted as one by one, the Beefeater family is cannibalized. *Yeccch*. *Disgusting.*

What about Stephanie? Stephanie was a photography student at Michigan State University when she created MeatMation as a class project. "I remember when I first hung this exhibit. The whole room was silent..." she says. No kidding Stephanie.

MeatMation has to be read to believed. And throughout its cavalcade of cannibalism, you'll find gruesome, color photographs of the family. OK, so it isn't exactly Jim Hensen's Muppets (unless Jim was a butcher) but it's definitely a site that you won't walk away from hungry (if you don't lose your appetite).

play with her food.

nally supposed to do a project on religion, so my whole class thought that I was going to be coming in with this religious photography project. I didn't know I was doing this until a couple of days before-hand. My friends are like, "What are you going to do??" "It's in my head man, I know what I'm going to do, it's OK." Once I thought of it, and what I needed to do, it was fine. I thought, "OK, let's see. Color, meat. Meat's red, you know, good color." And the only way for me to preserve my sculpture was through photography, because you can't really sculpt out of ground beef and then leave it laying around. So, I said that's it. I'm going to sculpt ground beef for my picture. So I decided I needed a story. I decided I would dress a character out of meat and have him go through and eat his entire family. And then I'm going to go on and have him eat himself, but I didn't get that far. The lights were really hot, and the meat was beginning to cook before my eyes. My house was starting to stink.

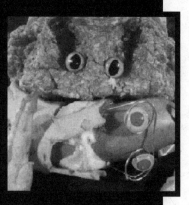

WWW: *How did the class react?*

SR: I came in with it matted on blood-red board. I came in and set it all out. Everyone was walking around looking at the class projects, and the whole class ended up in front of my pictures. "This is yours??? Stephanie." My teacher thought that because everyone had stopped at my project, we should discuss it first.

They wanted to know where this came from. "Who the hell has been in my classroom all this time?" My teacher really liked it.

WWW: *What kind of feedback have you gotten?*

SR: The ones that didn't like this surprised me. I really did this because I was a vegetarian for over a year. I was from a small town where hunting is bigger than Christmas. I would walk into our rec room and my brother would be sitting there with a deer head, practicing his taxidermy.

Now I moved into school into a house filled with vegetarians. I didn't eat meat every day. I was going through a lot where everyone at home would never in a million years not think of eating meat, I mean every meal...meat... meat...meat. Then I was moved into a different community where they were appalled that I came from a family of hunters. So I was totally stuck in the middle. I basically took it as a funny thing. Like, I'm not going to be all serious about it.

I'm just playing with meat ... that's all it is really. It's a funny thing when you think about it. It's something everyone sees every day but no one really thinks about it. Instead of looking at it as so serious and intense I just wanted to look at it in my own way. Hey, you know. We're all meat. And we all eat meat. So I guess we're going to eat each other really.

WWW: *Did you play with your food when you were a little kid?*
SR: When I got bored the first thing I'd do was play with my food. I don't get really grossed out about things. I'm from a small town, and I thought this was really hilarious.

WWW: *So, what's next?*
SR: I would love to keep working on this project, but I can't because I have no money. I'm not sure. I like to do things that have a sense of humor.

WWW: *Have you considered using other edible things as our medium?*
SR: Yeah, I've looked into it. I've also thought of a bunch of skits for the "Beefies." Yeah, I have. I think it's so fun. But I had

to cut it short because under the lights the meat was beginning to turn brown, and everyone in the house was beginning to yell at me.

WWW: *What kind of advice would you offer people who wanted to do a truly weird site?*
SR: Stick with the original plan. Don't listen to anyone else because … when I came up with this it was all in my head … I saw exactly what I wanted. I just blocked everything out. I came up with something I'm really proud of.

WWW: *What kind of problems did you encounter?*
SR: The meat was really hard to work with. Whenever I'd maneuver the characters, chunks would fall out.

WWW: *Why is Mr. Beefy made of part hamburger and part chicken?*
SR: I just needed him to be more pliable. I needed emotion in his face.

WWW: *Is there a deeper meaning to this site?*
SR: I think we take for granted what everyday life is. I don't think we really stop to think about what we consume and everything. And it's so second nature to us. Every day it's second nature to eat bacon for breakfast, and pigs for lunch, and cows for dinner. These things are part of our environment. We look at them as food, and we don't look at them as friends. Some people do see these animals as friends, and so we're eating family.

body parts

It's amazing how important interface design is to all of us. Imagine if you jumped into a car and DIDN'T find a steering wheel or accelerator pedal. Or if you reached for your refrigerator door and couldn't find a handle. Or if you went to program your VCR, and could actually do it EASILY! The Web has become a haven for all kinds of new interfaces, from virtual environments to toolbars with icons to human bodies. That's right—human bodies!

Witness the Clickable Anthony Web Page. Instead of looking for hypertext links or buttons, you click on Anthony's body.

CLICKABLE ANTHONY

http://www-groups.dcs.st-and.ac.uk/~meo/Anthony/

CLICK on an elbow, and you're launched to Professor Biceps and His Wonderful Babies, a totally twisted kind of child abuse?

CLICK on a foot, and you're at the Feet Cam.

CLICK on Anthony's face, and you'll discover that it's been turned into an interface of its own.

CLICK on his nose, and you'll jump to the Click & Sniff page, where a whole new kind of media is being explored. (Unfortunately, my allergies were bad the day I tried!)

CLICK on his lips, and you'll find yourself at the front door of the Virtual Kissing Booth.

As you read through the site, you discover that it originated as a big joke that was played on Anthony R. Huggett by his friends shortly after he was married. According to someone, "After years of failed sharking [is that British slang for something exotic?], his friends figured his wife would appreciate having a semi-nude image (he's not wearing a shirt) of her hubby passed onto a medium where most of the world could take a gander."

For hours of fun for the whole family, find Clickable Anthony—and just start clicking.

interview with **MARK ORZECHOWSKI**

WWW: What was your inspiration or, maybe more accurately, what drove you to create this site?
MO: We [Anthony's friends] first met in 1990 while studying at Cambridge University. We teased Anthony for many years about not being able to get a girlfriend; then one day last year, he suddenly announced to us all (via e-mail) that he was engaged! After the initial shock, we started to hatch ideas for his stag night. Somebody suggested exposing Anthony to ridicule on the World Wide Web. We found a particularly apt photograph of him proudly wearing just a pair of Lycra shorts, digitized it, and so The Clickable Anthony was born.

WWW: Were there any accomplices?
MO: There were about a dozen of us collaborating in total, but special thanks must go to Paul Johnson for getting the page working in the first place and to Ben Soares for other technical stuff.

WWW: What are your goals?
MO: To cause the maximum global embarrassment to Anthony, of course!

WWW: How much effort did it take to create this page?
MO: It was quite time consuming to start with—we had to learn how to use imagemaps and CGI scripts as well as provide all the links to various parts of Anthony's anatomy. It also takes a lot of effort to keep the page in good working order—by the very nature of the Internet, pages are coming and going all the time, and I've had to keep the links up to date.

WWW: Where and how do you go about gathering your content?
MO: Mainly search engines (Lycos in particular), but also through the various collections of bizarre pages to be found on the Web.

WWW: What kind of reaction did your friends have to this site when you first told them about it?
MO: They all love it! Even Anthony. I think he's enjoying all the attention.

WWW: Your relatives?
MO: I haven't told my mum—I think she might be shocked.

WWW: How has the Web-wandering community reacted to it?
MO: Very well, on the whole. The page has a visitors' book, and it's had a lot of favorable comments. Anthony now seems very popular with the girls— he's received several proposals of marriage!

WWW: What's next?
MO: The Clickable Myfanwy? [That's Anthony's bride-to-be; she's Welsh.] I don't think she'd be too happy with the idea, though.

WWW: What kind of person would you like to attract to your site?
MO: I'm sure Anthony would like to attract stunning blondes in their early 20s, though again, Myfanwy might object.

WWW: Have you learned any lessons from doing something this bizarre?
MO: That a lot of other people have also put some very strange pages on the Web— fortunately for me!

WWW: What kind of words of wisdom can you give other lost souls who have this itch they just gotta scratch to put out a truly weird Web wonder?
MO: Scratch away! No, better still—click!

clickable anthony

Spend any real time surfing the Web, and you'll be amazed at the vast array of home pages out there. From the incredibly functional, such as Mapquest; to the tasteful, like Salon; to the disturbing, like Dan's Gallery of the Grotesque. Yet among this motley group, one of the more unusual is Internet in a Baby. You'll find a portrait of a rather pleasant-looking young boy, and you can click on various parts of his body to navigate to various areas of the Web.

I N T E R N

http://www.wideweb.com/baby/

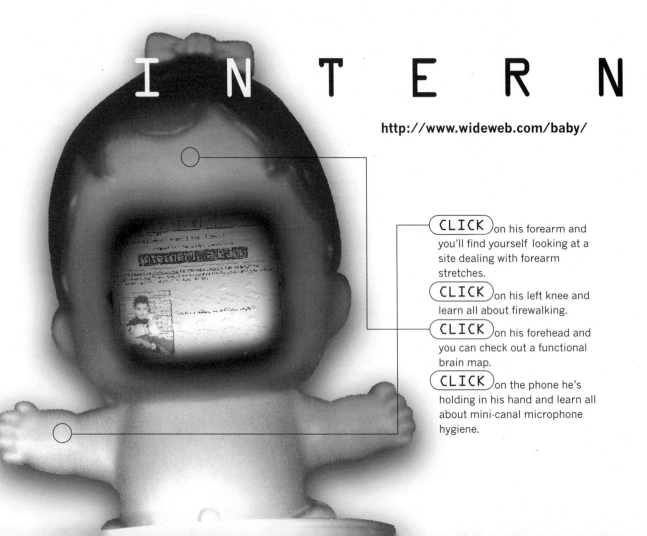

(CLICK) on his forearm and you'll find yourself looking at a site dealing with forearm stretches.

(CLICK) on his left knee and learn all about firewalking.

(CLICK) on his forehead and you can check out a functional brain map.

(CLICK) on the phone he's holding in his hand and learn all about mini-canal microphone hygiene.

E T **baby**
i n a

The motivation for Internet in a Baby is claimed to
have been the popular Internet program "Internet in
a Box".™ Will this become the interface of choice in
the Web of the future? Has Bill Gates already approached the creator to explore acquisition possibilities for Windows '97? Probably not. Nonetheless, it's
definitely unique.

interview with **RICHARD KASHDAN**

WWW: What was your inspiration for this site?

RK: I wanted a Web page about myself but was a little shy about including a real picture of myself, so I used a picture of me as a child instead. At about the same time, I read an article about how to use image maps to make a picture clickable. For no other reason than to learn the concepts in this article, I made a map of all the parts of my childhood portrait and linked them to sites that seemed relevant. You can still see this original page at http://www.wideweb.com/rkashdan.

Later I got the idea to turn this into a joke page with no direct reference to me. I copied the "rkashdan" page into a new directory, kept the picture and the image map, but changed all the wording. This became Internet in a Baby.

WWW: What are your goals?

RK: None, really, except to watch the hit counter go up as fast as possible.

WWW: How much effort did it take to create this page?

RK: Many, many, hours—and I still work on it several hours a month to update the links from the parts of the baby picture.

WWW: Where and how do you gather your content?

RK: I am always on the lookout for Web pages that make sense as links from the baby picture. If I don't stumble over any good ones for a long period of time, then I go to the search engines and look for suitable sites.

WWW: What kind of reaction did your friends have to this site?
RK: They thought it was pretty stupid until the site was made Cool Site of the Day for April 2, 1995, and then they were proud to know me.

WWW: Your relatives?
RK: I haven't told them about it. Would you?

WWW: How has the Web-wandering community reacted to it?
RK: I have a feedback form on the page for comments. The most common one by far is "Why do you call it 'Internet in a Baby'? That's no baby, it looks like a young child." The second most common is, "I was trying to find pages about naming my new baby, but the search engine gave me your page."

WWW: How do you feel now that it's up?
RK: I'm starting to get bored with it. It was more fun for the first few months. But there is an interesting side benefit from having a fairly popular Web site: I can run my own statistics about browsers and operating system usage. My counter program keeps statistics on which brand of browser the user had and what operating system, so I can, for example, prove to my Mac bigot friends that Macs do not have 50% of Internet usage (it's more like 15%) and that the Microsoft Internet Explorer is not overtaking Netscape.

WWW: What's next?
RK: I have a new page called Phone Trips at http://www.wideweb.com/phonetrips. I have a great idea for another joke page, but I don't want to give it away yet.

WWW: Have you learned any lessons from doing something this bizarre?
RK: Bizarre? What do you mean? Do you think it's bizarre to have a Web page that links Web sites to body parts on a baby picture?

WWW: What words of wisdom can you give other lost souls who want to create a Web page?
RK: Learn HTML coding by hand rather than relying on fancy editing tools. Look around for cheap ISPs to host your page. The hardest part is publicity. Here is how I got started: I really liked Glen Davis's Cool Site of the Day (http://cool.infi.net) and I followed his link every time I signed on to Netscape. I really wanted Internet in a Baby to be his cool site. I found one of those sites that lets you send someone an e-mail postcard with a picture and a small amount of text. I sent one to Glen saying:

Roses are red

Violets are blue

If you make http://www. wideweb.com/baby your cool site of the day

I will surely love you.

That's all I did. Believe it or not, about two days later I started getting a bunch of feedback forms in a row, I looked at the Cool Site of the Day page, and there I was! The Cool Site link gave me thousands of hits per day for a few days. Internet in a Baby now appears in many other lists of humorous Web sites, but almost all of that derived from being Cool Site of the Day.

WWW: What kind of person would you like to attract to a site like this?
RK: I really don't care, as long as they add 1 to the hit counter. It's also nice if they send feedback.

WAY OF
EXPLODING
HEA

http://www.king.net/gilmore/head/

It's interesting when you wander the weirder side of the Web. You find lots of sites that seem to dwell on food. Lots that are based on some perversion of religion. And lots that have basically the same sense of humor as a fourteen-year-old boy—in other words, GROSS IS GREAT.

The Exploding Head Page fits this description to a T—and adds a hefty dose of humorous commentary on top. Watch as presidential candidate Bob Dole blows his top—*quite literally*—when he witnesses the depravity of the Exploding Head Page.

Or Rush Limbaugh, as he crashes his cranium. Or even the ultimate Prince of Darkness, Bill Gates, as he has massive cerebral general protection error.

If it's depth, this site doesn't really have it. If it's relevance, it must have had something, because the FBI once paid a visit. That's right—in January 1996, agents of the FBI showed up at Gilmore's place, demanded to see the images, and began asking serious questions about why one of his vict—ah—characters was Senator Bob Dole. After some carefully worded reasoning and another meeting down at the FBI office, the issue was dropped. Still, Gilmore came away with a valuable lesson learned.

So kids, try to learn a lesson from all this: DON'T *(&^ WITH BOB DOLE. And don't try to use your home scanner powers to explode the heads of presidential candidates.

And for the record: I don't wish Bob Dole any harm. I hope he lives a long and fruitful life, happily exploiting the masses, oppressing the downtrodden, and taking huge "contributions" from corporate-funded PACs, until he dies a peaceful natural death WHEN HIS HEAD EXPLODES oh god no scratch that last part!

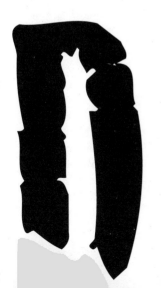

interview with **GILMORE**

WWW: What drove you to create this site?

G: Well, my friend Quinn and I were sitting around watching TV, drinking cheap beer, and doing what we do best, which is bitch at the TV and get angry about how stupid everyone is. Quinn mentioned, "Wouldn't it be great if there was a TV channel where everyone's head exploded?" We laughed about that, and the next day at work (I'm a Web designer) I decided to try my hand at a few exploding heads. Next thing I knew, I had a Web page.

WWW: Were there any accomplices—or are you the only one that can be held liable?

G: As above, Quinn (http://www.vv.com/~quinn) inspired me to make the page.

WWW: How much effort was it?

G: Not a lot—a couple Saturdays goofing about with Photoshop and there it was. Though there was some skill involved in making the explosions interesting.

WWW: Where and how do you gather your content?

G: Went through *Newsweek* looking for pictures of people who needed their heads exploded.

WWW: What kind of reaction did your friends have to the site?

G: "Exploding WHAT? Gimme the address!" *howls of laughter*

WWW: Your relatives?

G: My dad's a minister, so my parents had, um, mixed reactions to all the publicity surrounding the page. My mom told me the choir director at our church came to my dad's office after church one day to ask if he "was aware of his son's subversive activities." Hee hee!

WWW: The local police?
G: No reaction, but the FBI didn't appreciate it too much, which you can read about on the Web page.

WWW: Have you heard back from the victims—er—subjects of your little animations? How did they react?
G: Ahh, if only, if only. Still waiting for mail from good ol' Bill.

WWW: How has the Web-wandering community reacted to it?
G: I've gotten a lot of positive feedback about the page; everyone seems to love it. I suppose the kind of people who hate tasteless humor just never end up there.

WWW: What's next?
G: Believe me, I've been asking myself that same question. Everyone keeps discouraging me from doing the "Leprechauns Are Fags" Fact Page.

WWW: Have you learned any lessons from doing something this bizarre?
G: Absolutely. The media only gives attention to stupid things and not to anything of substance. The amount of time the media wasted reporting on me was staggering, considering how many important things go on behind the scenes that no one EVER hears about.

WWW: What words of wisdom can you offer potential Web publishers?
G: Do it! Do it! That's what makes the Web rich and beautiful— not idiots like Microsoft and IBM putting up their giant useless Web extravaganzas, but each Websurfer sharing their little piece of odd entertainment or information.

WWW: What kind of person would you like to attract to your site?
G: Everyone. Really, though, I'm not interested in attracting anyone—if people get a kick out of the site, that's great. The only people I would want to attract might be either (1) beautiful nymphomaniacs or (2) people with big sacks of money to give to talented Web designers.

Doctor Froggy's Medical

http://www.rain.org/~davidh/drfroggy.htm

A lot of people on the World Wide Web have a really bizarre sense of humor. And along with them are a whole range of Web pages that make you chuckle—nervously.

One of the best of these is Dr. Froggy's Medical Marvels Page, which focused, when I discovered it, on the heartbreak of hemorrhoids and how to permanently rid yourself of them. This graphically rich (in more ways than one) site begins by defining whether you really do have a problem with the "mondo butt boulders," as Dr. Froggy so aptly puts it:

> Do you perform that obscene little dance—the Cheek-Squeakin' Boogie—trying to relieve the nasty ol' itch that always seems to flare up the minute you walk into a crowded cafeteria? Do you spend entire afternoons sitting on one of those stupid little blow-up donuts wishing it didn't feel like there was a three-day-old taco wedged between your buttocks? Have you ever awakened on the floor ... only to discover that your hemorrhoids are still in bed? Do you try to recall the exact moment your bathroom habits

Marvels Page

made the tragic change over from a smile and a wipe to a grimace and a minuscule Tucks pad? Does the word "Speedo" make you cringe? Do you avoid frequenting public places so you won't cause an outbreak of mass projectile vomiting in the event you accidentally break wind and make that awful, wretched noise that sounds like a troupe of naked, over-amped midgets flogging each other with slices of wet bologna? [Eeeew!] Are your hemorrhoids so cruel they hang out the bottom of your pants leg and drag on the cement when you walk? If you answered "Yes!" to any of the above questions, then you need (shout it with me now!) Doctor Froggy's Instant Hemorrhoid Removal Kit!

The page goes on to describe the contents of the Removal Kit and how to use them. To be perfectly honest, this page was entertaining, funny, and seriously disturbing. So much so, that I'll let you all check it out yourself.

 interview with **DAVID HOPKINS**

WWW: How much effort have you put into this page?
DH: Three weeks total for concept and creation. And I discover stuff to add just by listening to people.

WWW: What kind of reaction did you friends have to the site?
DH: Uncontrollable laughter!

WWW: Your relatives?
DH: I don't know. They don't call much anymore since they discovered they could relate rather closely to some of the things present at the Doctor Froggy site.

WWW: The local police?
DH: I think they use a different type of communications package. Although I think Doctor Froggy could definitely help lighten their mood!

WWW: How has the Web-wandering community reacted to it?
DH: Overwhelming "Thumbs up!!" is the general consensus.

WWW: Have you learned any lessons from doing something this bizarre?
DH: Yes. That placing a humor page with a direct link to your home page is a great idea!

WWW: Any words of wisdom for other Web publishers?
DH: Go for it!

WWW: What kind of person would you like to attract to a site like this?
DH: Anyone with a healthy [ouch] sense of humor.

doctor froggy's medical marvels page

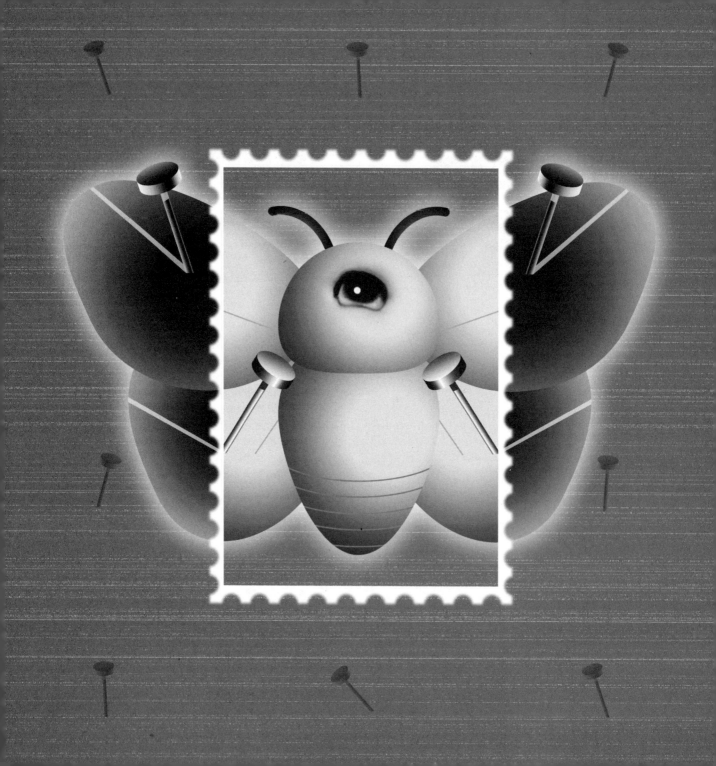

collections

collections

Coochi!!
Coochi!!

Cheezy Cultural Primer

http://204.137.163.12:80/homepgs/superchris/

I have to admit it: I love cheese! I'm not talking about solid food prepared from the pressed curd of milk. I'm talking about cheese as in cheesy. I relish the chance to watch infomercials about products like the FH2000 (Fake Hair 2000) or Suck-n-Vac.

I've always been a closet fan of TV shows like The Brady Bunch and the weirder episodes of Lost in Space. And some of my fondest vacation memories are of visiting hallowed halls of cheese like The Corn Palace and Wall Drug (both in the geographical center of cheese and cornball, South Dakota).

That's why I was so excited when I stumbled onto the Cheezy Cultural Primer. Finally, someone was taking the time to promote this uniquely American phenomenon (OK, OK—so Sweden had ABBA). From this home page, you have the option of heading off into Dubious Art & Culture, where Cultural Tips from Jesus link you to some of the cheesiest Kultural Kreations ("K" is very cheesy) ever, from TV shows like Scooby Doo and Starsky and

Hutch to musical merriment from icons like Kiss and Tony Orlando & Dawn (who is still appearing, minus Dawn, in his own club in the new Capital of Cheese: Branson, Missouri). There's even a link to that Latin Lulu, Charo!

I'm haunted by my first memories of Charo. When I was a child, I'd rush home from school past the other neighborhood kids playing baseball in the street. I'd grab a package of those pasteurized processed cheese nibbles (the kind that came in individually wrapped cellophane, like candy), and throw myself down on the couch for the most glamorous part of my day: the Merv Griffin Show! I can still remember the chills I got when the Dunes Hotel sign first appeared on the screen and Merv made his suave entrance to the set. I dreamed of running away to Las Vegas as the day's guests were announced. Who would it be today? Totie Fields? Joey Heatherton? Liberace? Of course, all the time I'd be hoping against hope that it would be Charo.

Other areas of wonder at this Cathedral of Cheese include Way Mega Cheese, Great Cultural Heroes, a broad selection of Erotic Links, and special sections such as the Charo page mentioned above and Technology, Testosterone, and the Internet (a serious commentary on the cheesiest of all cultural crazes, the Communications Decency Act).

The Cheezy Cultural Primer is only an introduction to the world of cheese. Through its vast range of links, the more aesthetically adventurous can explore many great cultural treasures overlooked in the more mainstream art circles. Who knows, maybe someday a visit to the National Museum will find exhibits of all that cheesy stuff that makes this country great.

 interview with **CHRIS MADONNA**

WWW: What was your inspiration for this site?

CM: Growing up in the seventies, surrounded by an explosion of cheezy pop culture, I've always been drawn to the kitsch aesthetic. I feel that lowbrow mass culture is the truest and most accurate barometer of a society. Our late twentieth-century psyches have been shaped more by Rhoda Morgenstern and Scooby Doo than Shakespeare or Freud. I set out to create a Web site that would explore and celebrate this aspect of our culture.

WWW: Were there any accomplices?

CM: I'm a solitary criminal.

WWW: What are your goals?

CM: My main goal is to educate and enlighten the Internet masses on the aesthetics of cheeze and tastelessness.

WWW: How much effort was this page?

CM: Obviously, no great art is created without attendant pain and anguish, and the Cheezy Cultural Primer is certainly no exception. My main problem was and is sorting through the mildly tasteless faux cheeze (e.g., Deborah Harry and Madonna) and pointing my audience to the timeless kitsch of cultural gurus such as Charo and José Feliciano.

Illustrating this subtle but crucial difference is a constant but rewarding struggle.

WWW: Where and how do you gather your content?

CM: I surf the Net for cheeze on an average of three to five hours a day and clip photos from old magazines and newspapers. I use

my scanner as a guer-
rilla kitsch weapon.

**WWW: What kind
of reaction did
your friends have
to this site?**
CM: Reactions have
varied from disbelief
to delight. (My first
shrine, El Mundo de
Charo, has generated
hundreds of fan mes-
sages from around the
world).

WWW: The local police?
CM: None yet...but
Seattle cops are pretty
kewl, n'est-ce pas?

**WWW: How has the
Web-wandering com-
munity reacted to it?**
CM: I've received e-
mail responses from
around the world
praising my efforts,
and even received an
indecent proposal
from a college dean
somewhere in Canada
(I think it was
Saskatchewan).

WWW: What's next?
CM: To paraphrase the
late Karen Carpenter,
"I've only just
begun..."

WALL O' SHAME

Editor's Notes

I've always believed that, no matter how bizarre fiction can get, it pales when compared to reality. And on the "Weird" Wide Web, no place bears this out with quite the effect of the Wall O' Shame, a collection that, as the creator put it, "attempts to characterize the erosion of our world by displaying true stories and tidbits that are just too nonlinear."

KILLER GUIDE DOG
Four dead, who's next?
Simulated Press

This is putting it mildly! "Lucky Dog" relates the tale of a hapless guide dog for the blind who has been responsible for the deaths of all four of his owners so far. He led his first owner in front of a bus, the second off a pier, actually pushed the third off a railway platform in front of a train (accidentally, of course), and he led the fourth into the middle of a crowded intersection before leaving him there and running to safety. You might think those in charge of this dog would decide that guiding the blind was not the best career choice, but with an airy "Guide dogs are difficult to train these days," they give him to some other hapless owner. Are they warning the new owner about this dog's past accomplishments? "No. It would make them nervous and would make Lucky nervous. And when Lucky gets nervous, he's liable to do something silly."

Mummified Woman Found After 3 Years!

Conversely, "Immortality" tells the story of a Swedish woman who passed away. Because her computer dutifully paid her bills even after her death, her body wasn't discovered for THREE YEARS!

AN UNBELIEVABLE SITE TO SEE!
by the author

Besides hair-raising stories, Wall O' Shame also features a number of clippings from other publications, including a look at the Waterproof Home of the Future (believe it or not, I actually saw a video once on this concept with a home that cleaned itself, much like a dishwasher does!), and under the title "Would you like fries with that?" a photograph of the Polytron, which will reduce an "'entire mouse to a soup-like homogenate in under 30 seconds.'" Hmm, I always wondered what those fast food restaurants were using to make those extra-thick milk shakes.

interview with **DAN BORNSTEIN**

> "...true stories and tidbits that are just too nonlinear."

WWW: What drove you to create this site?
DB: Pure whim. I did it before the Web was discovered by commercial interests, and I thought it would be nice to add to the signal level of the new frontier.

WWW: What are your goals?
DB: To entertain. To have fun.

WWW: How much effort was this page?
DB: Not a lot. I don't do flashy graphics or Java or junk like that. I'm much more interested in pure content.

WWW: Where and how do you gather your content?
DB: Anything and everything is fair game, although since the explosion I've been worrying more about copyright issues. I think I'm safe under the fair-use doctrine, but perhaps AP sees things a different way.

WWW: What kind of reaction did your friends have to this site? Your relatives?
DB: They all pretty much like it. It's not really controversial.

WWW: How has the Web-wandering community reacted to it?
DB: Mostly positively, although the occasional vocal right-wing type gets pissed off at the "NRA Logic" story.

WWW: How do you feel now that it's up?
DB: Fine, but unfortunately it gnaws at me that I don't have enough time to do a proper job of maintaining it. (I guess if I were motivated enough, I could get it to a stage where I could sell out, but that's not really where my interests lie.)

WWW: What's next?
DB: Slowly adding to and evolving the site in my copious free time.

WWW: Have you learned any lessons from doing something this bizarre?
DB: There are a lot of other weirdos out there; it's nice to know you're not alone.

WWW: What words of wisdom can you give others who want to publish on the Web?
DB: Go for it. The cost of entry is so small that the only reason not to do it is lack of motivation.

WWW: What kind of person would you like to attract to a site like this?
DB: Anyone with an off-beat sense of humor.

wall o' shame

Mirsky's Worst of the Web

http://mirsky.com/wow/

Since its early days in 1993, the World Wide Web has become home to literally millions of Web pages of every description. Over the first couple of years, a number of sites sprang up to salute those who excelled in this new medium. At times, it seemed that we would break our arms patting ourselves on the back.

Then came Mirsky (his real name is hidden to protect the guilty), who wanted to focus on the darker side of the Web, and so created Mirsky's Worst of the Web. It's an extensive guide to thousands of Web pages that probably never should have been, all reviewed with a witty and biting commentary that only someone like Mirsky could pull off.

On a recent visit to The Worst, I discovered the following gems: One page merely said "Photos of My Tractors" and had six links. Mirsky worried that there would actually be people out there who would come back every week, hoping to find a new tractor added.

A strange page talking about the Corn God was attributed to a man who was contacted by God and extraterrestrials and told to break the code of another language overlaid on the English language. Mirsky claimed he believed it but also thought it was a great waste of time. I agree.

Still another was a photo exhibit based on the Art of Menstruation. No more needs to be said about this one.

Of a page that only says, "This page will soon offer help to those who need it," Mirsky writes, "This page is giving false hope to people in Bosnia, Liberia, Central America, along with millions and millions of desperate, war-torn and impoverished others, nationally and world-wide!"

A link to McDonald's Adult section comments, "They could at least compensate for this with a little nudity."

A link to a page called the Confessional, which is one person's confessions. Ahem...I don't know about you, but I've never really been into listening in on other people's guilt.

Mirsky's latest also includes a link to a proposal for a dating service for men with hairy backs.

Spend a while visiting Mirsky's most recommended sites and you begin to realize there are lots of people doing lots of truly awful Web sites out there. But Mirsky's effort goes further than just highlighting the Worst of the Web. He/She is showing just how free and open the Web is. Anybody with an idea, whether it be a beautifully executed experience or a collection of tractor photographs, can hang their shingle for all the world to see. And I, for one, (and probably Mirsky, for another) would fight to keep the Web that way.

interview with **MIRSKY**

WWW: What drove you to create this site?
M: It was Fate and the Lord God Almighty that lead me to publish my work online. However, I'm an atheist and a cynic, so I could be wrong.

WWW: Are you the only one that can be held liable?
M: I've done it all myself, but there were a number of people I wanted as accomplices. However, they were robbing banks, committing fraud, and so on. I didn't think they'd be interested.

WWW: How much work is it to find the worst sites?
M: Probably a lot more than it takes to be a sewer worker. That's why I'm thinking of switching.

WWW: Do you enjoy it?
M: Sometimes. It depends whether my cat is digging her claws into my lap.

WWW: What kind of reaction did your friends have to this site?
M: Most stopped being friends with me. But I think something else must have been bothering them.

WWW: Your relatives?
M: They were pissed, too. The association of the name Mirsky with stuff that is the worst has caused two family businesses to fail.

WWW: How has the Web-wandering community reacted to it? Any testimonials?
M: Mostly favorable responses: "This doesn't suck that bad!" is one I always cherish. Anonymous guest users have a great way with words.

WWW: Have you gotten any reactions from those sites you write about? Any nasty e-mail? Any ticking packages?
M: No ticking packages, but I have gotten a death threat. But I figure, once I'm dead, I shouldn't get any more.

WWW: What is it you hope that this site will achieve?
M: My goal has remained unchanged since I started the site: to make enough money to buy my own clothes.

WWW: What's next?
M: Probably unemployment.

WWW: What are your hopes, your dreams ... your nightmares?
M: My hopes, dreams, and nightmares are all sexual. Hey, I thought this was a family book!

WWW: Have you learned any lessons from doing something this bizarre?
M: Not really. But I once learned something from drinking a can of motor oil. Unfortunately, I can't remember what it was.

WWW: What words of wisdom can you give other potential Web authors?
M: I don't really have anything to say to them. But if I had a gun, I'd shoot them.

WWW: What kind of person would you like to attract to a site like this?
M: Someone with no arms, no legs, no sight, and no hearing. In order to do that, my site's got to be really, really good.

food

BUBBA'S BBQ CHIP

COLLEC

On the web you'll find that people get their jollies by collecting all sorts of things: barf bags, squashed bugs, Spam…even BBQ potato chips. Bubba's BBQ Chip Collection goes further than just a moldy collection of potato slices; it actually provides some interesting insight into a Great American Foodstuff—the potato chip.

As Bubba describes his quest:

> This particular quest began when I lived for four years in Indiana and began to miss some of the simple pleasures of Texas life. I began collecting Texas catalogs, and before I knew it, I had ordered a case of Bob's Texas Style Chips. My roommate admitted that these were indeed the best chips he had tasted, but he recommended Snyder BBQ Chips from Pennsylvania. At that point, the quest for the best BBQ chips had begun. Wherever I went, I sought out the regional BBQ chips. And I seek still…

He uses a rather unusual icon to rate his chips—namely, how well they will spoil dinner ("Eat a Chip, Ruin a Meal")—and claims this is because his mother always used to scold him about eating chips and ruining his dinner. Scroll down the page and you'll find a vast array of chips that he has tried and a list of his favorites.

The three top winners, in Bubba's opinion, are Bickel's, Bob's Texas Style, and Zapp's (which of course has its own home page at http://www.noconnect.com/shopping/zapps/zapps.htm).

Now, if you consider yourself a lover of BBQ potato chips (no corn chips, PLEASE!) just drop by Bubba's home page and see if you can help him out.

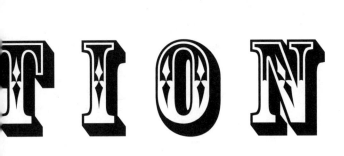

 interview with **GARY BEASON**

WWW: *What was your inspiration or, maybe more accurately, what drove you to create this site?*

GB: I had a chip obsession long before the idea for a website. I actually started the website as a way to get others to help me find the potato chips. I had been collecting the chips just from my own travels. Then, about five years ago, I posted to a newsgroup (re: foods) and got some response. When I finally had access to some storage space and a Web server, I put the collection online to try to entice others to submit recommendations and reviews. So far, it's worked pretty well.

WWW: *Were there any accomplices?*

GB: Not really. My girlfriend helped by scanning potato chip bags.

My roommate, Jeff Baker, contributed the idea of junk food reviews and the elusiveness of the perfect chip.

WWW: *What are your goals?*

GB: For this page? Well, I'd like to start getting more chips and have state-by-state (even country-by-country) breakdowns. Lately, however, the chip suggestions have been slowing down.

WWW: *How much effort did it take to create this page?*

GB: Initially, not much, because it was just text only. But then I added some graphics and reviews. It's a bit of work to write the reviews, respond to the e-mail (which can be quite a job), scan and upload graphics, and continue to eat new chips.

WWW: Where and how do you go about gathering your content?

GB: I first started collecting the chips as I went to states adjacent to Indiana, where I lived for five years. As I told friends about my search, they helped out by bringing me bags from their trips as well. (Although some friends were a bit fuzzy about the focus on BBQ chips—they brought corn chip aberrations and other flavors. Nonetheless, their efforts were encouraging.)

Then, when I went for a job interview in Seattle, I found some very different flavors, like "alder smoked flavor." After that, I then hit every vending machine at every airport. (Suddenly, I began anticipating layovers...one man's burden and all that jazz.) I accumulated about 30 or so different chips this way. Now, I rely on the kindness of strangers who share a love for the potato chip.

WWW: What kind of reaction did your friends have to this site when you first told them about it?

GB: They laughed. It is pretty ridiculous. I knew that. But, as people have visited it, suggested chips, and even written about it, they're still amused—but they offer suggestions for designing it and such.

WWW: Your relatives?

GB: My mother thinks it's silly, but she's intrigued by the Internet (she's 73 years old). Oh, and she doesn't think much of my quoting her. :)

Most of my family is mildly amused. The cat doesn't care; she thinks people are pretty inane anyway.

WWW: How has the Web-wandering community reacted to it?

GB: So far, the reactions have been very good. I don't track number of visits or stuff like that. But I have had about 100 e-mail responses to it in the last year.

It's funny...more than once, people have invested me with some sort of expertise, whether it be about BBQ in general, chips, or sales. One company wrote me and asked for recommendations about flavor.

WWW: How do you feel now that it's up?

GB: Very self-amused.

WWW: Have you learned any lessons from doing something this bizarre?

GB: Well, it's not that weird or bizarre. I've seen what you other people are doing. And it's just twisted. I have also learned that, although I probably need to get a life, there are many more people with just as much time on their hands. I'm amazed by the people who take the time to send me mail or even find the site in the first place.

WWW: What kind of words of wisdom can you give other lost souls who have this itch they just gotta scratch to put out a truly weird Web wonder?

GB: Don't do it if you don't want to—or can't—maintain it.

WWW: What kind of person would you like to attract to a site like this?

GB: Bring me your tired...no, wait, that's been done.

I would like for everyone everywhere who has ever obsessed about finding the right grill, car, or whatever—who has ever searched for that platonic ideal of anything that brings them the most pleasure—I want these people who enjoy tirelessly searching and comparing to come by and visit.

I especially want visits from people who have new chips for me to try!

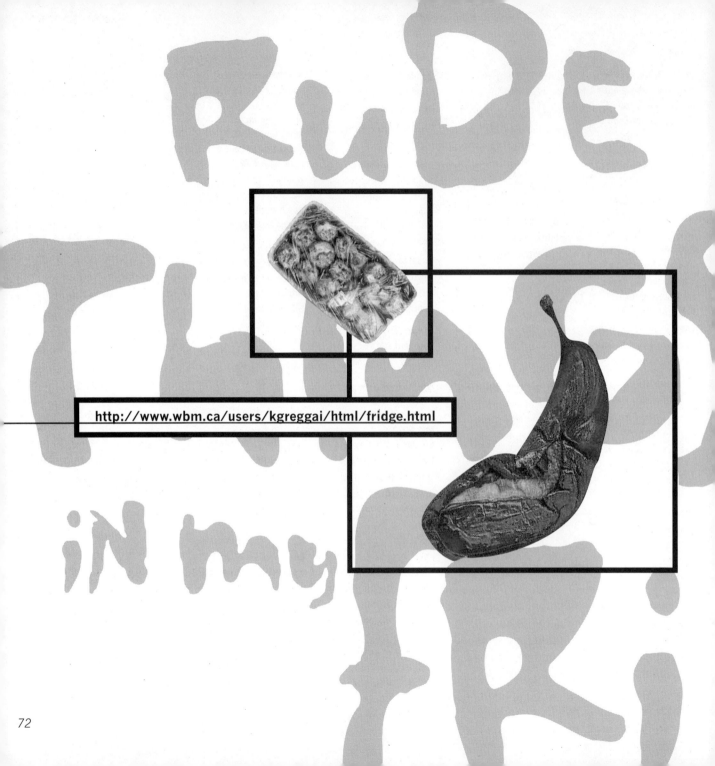

RUDE
THINGS
iN my
FRi

http://www.wbm.ca/users/kgreggai/html/fridge.html

I used to think I was a bit messy ... OK, I was a down and dirty SLOB. I bragged that I had been approached by the local biotech firm about my refrigerator, which they claimed was the ideal environment to create life forms, vastly superior to any petri dish. I used to qualify for Superfunds. It really used to freak out my neighbors when, every now and then, a nondescript government van would show up full of guys in white spacesuits who would trudge in and out of my apartment, carefully carrying plastic bags of stuff. My microwave resembles Marvel Caverns. My bedroom closet ... well, you begin to get the idea. I used to think I was seriously sloppy ... until I discovered Kevin's page. I spent a few moments checking out the high-resolution, brilliant color images of the inside of Kevin's fridge and realized—I'm an AMATEUR!

Kevin has this thing about leaving things in his Kenmore a little beyond their expiration dates—like years! And he's developed a fascination with the transformations that result. So where does he put pictures of the latest tasteless trophies? Why, on the World Wide Web for all to see, of course! He describes himself:

> I'm a pig, the lowest of the male species. My shorts can breakdance in my basement, the cats sit on a mound of what might have been cat litter, and my fridge...My god, there's something alive in there.

Using an elegant page design, with flies resting along the left side of the screen, Kevin doesn't actually show you anything on the home page. He just taunts you to "open the fridge." Hmm ... let's see what appeared in April...

> My wiener has a first name, it's D-E-C-A-Y! Yes—4 wieners from 4 major producers in the world and only this brand (withheld) decomposed. The others just got real dark. Funny though, they didn't stink. Still smelled fresh. Maybe if I had removed the wrapper ...

Not only does this rather questionable culinary delight appear in full color, but there's also a musical accompaniment. You'll also find links to some of the fetid food fun from previous months: seriously MUSHEDrooms from May 1995, something that may have been a banana in November, and so on through the "Disgust of the Month Club."

You'll also find how other humans have reacted to the site, from those who praise him for perpetuating the stereotype that most bachelors have "moved back UP the evolutionary scale" to those with less complimentary comments.

One of my favorites was a little poetry:

> The smell is like a red, red rose, spreading its fragrant aroma throughout my kitchen. The sight is more beautiful than a blood red sunset, seen through the eyes of a moon goddess. Take me to your world of steamy delights, where I can be free to roam the wilderness and delight in the discovery of all its arcane inhabitants. Oh great fridge, I worship thy magnificent whiteness, and the ooze that cascades from above. I am your slave, dominate me with your rotting magnificence.

Of course, it helps that Kevin has a seriously twisted love of horror—to the extent that he maintains The Night Gallery, where it's Halloween 365 days a year!

The Fridge page has to be seen to be believed. Every month, a new substance joins the ranks of the rancid. Of course, because Kevin lives in Canada he doesn't have an EPA to help him clean up the place.

interview with **KEVIN GREGGAIN**

WWW: So, where did you first find the inspiration to create your Web site?

KG: Since birth, I've been different, obtuse, and somewhat wacko (according to my friends). My love for horror stems from a few movies I watched (which my mother tried to keep me from seeing). It was my morbid curiosity that brought me to exclaim to the cyberworld via my Web page. I love horror movies, books, and whatever else is gross and revolting. I guess I kinda get a thrill from it all.

WWW: How much work was it collecting the content?

KG: There have been many months I have spent over 170 hours creating, scanning, searching and, uh, well—playing. A lot of the ideas come from my macabre and morbid sense of humor, and some (recently) as suggestions from friends and associates who have now accepted me for who I am. I'm sort of the class cyberclown.

WWW: Have you always been this messy?

KG: Yup, almost since birth. A true bachelor, born and raised. I've tried help groups, supportive family members, resentful and complaining ex-wives, all with no success. My job is hairy, stressful, and action-packed. When I get home after a day's work, the last thing I want to do is "function" as some pseudo-normal housedude. I just toss my socks up on the lampshade, kick back, and power up my computer. As a side note, my computer desk is usually pretty clean.

WWW: How did people react to you putting up pictures of all the gross things in your fridge? Your friends? Your family? Your roommate?

KG: Well, my parents have always looked the other way and denied my existence. :) Seriously, at first most people just looked pretty grossed out. Now, they're eager to see my next month's nightmare and complain if I am late in posting the latest scan. My roommate is cool with the whole deal; he's even helped find me items that will "culture" into something colorful for my page.

WWW: What kind of deeper meaning can we find in this site?

KG: Well, it may not be obvious, but I'm not advertising for a wife, if that's what you mean. In essence, I may very well be putting up warning signs: "Look, rude bachelor computer geekoid!" or some-

thing. I guess it boils down to the fact that I just like to make people laugh. Any moron can tell jokes; I prefer to be remembered. When a Japanese magazine posted a short review about my fridge page, it made me aware that mold is international. Hey, maybe we can use these as some new way of communicating with other civilizations! :)

WWW: Do you think your fridge is that much more grotesque than other people's?

KG: In relation to the other bachelors of the world, no. But my fridge is the first in a series of mechanisms to let other bachelors "come out of the closet"—or fridge, as it were. We are men, hear us roar! Or something.

WWW: What's next?

KG: Well, between The Rude Things in My Fridge and the Body Music page, I think I've become crude

enough to shock most of the world as we know it. Trying to top the crudeness might be a little too much, even for the uncensored Web. My other interests involve horror, writing, and (gulp) romantic poetry, so I think I will obsess about another of my interests for a while.

WWW: What kind of tips can you provide a sloppy bachelor who revels in his fridge, and wants it to be as disgusting as yours?

KG: The ability to rot food is a skill that must be learned in stages, not unlike karate. A yellow belt may only let milk go sour in his fridge, whereas a true black belt can rot food as fast as you can say "Let's go out for McDonald's." A bachelor should not be embarrassed about his sloppiness, for we are the reason most grocery stores stay open late at night. ;)

WWW: What did you learn from doing this?

KG: The world can still laugh—even if it takes rotted food or rude body noises to wake people up from their daily lives. I learned to take life a little easier and not be so stressed (another reason I took on the Web pages). I also learned there are even rottener fridges out there. All the mail from Germany, Australia, Africa, and Japan confirms how eager people are to allow humor into their lives.

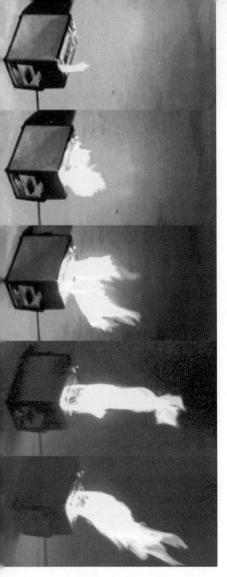

Do you like to play with your food? I mean, really *play* with your food? Well, Patrick R. Michaud does—in a big way. Patrick, an assistant professor of computer science at Texas A&M, has this thing about food products flaming and exploding and is the creator of both the Strawberry Pop-Tart Blow-Torches and the Sparking Seedless Grapes Page.

Patrick got his sadistic start when he discovered that grapes could be coerced into performing exciting dances with a little help from a microwave oven. After only a few seconds of intense radiation (compliments of the oven), the grapes begin to spark and flare. Patrick's "culinary entertainment" is fun for the whole family—and not only that, you can *eat* the props when you're done with 'em!

strawberry Pop-Tart Blow-torches

http://www.sci.tamucc.edu/~pmichaud/toast

Of course Patrick, being the academic type, performed this as a serious experiment and included the full detailed description of the procedure, the results, and any conclusions he and his fellow researchers could draw.

At this point, most bored scientists would be finished. They'd get back to their laboratory rats—or students, depending—and not give it another thought, except during exceptionally boring cocktail parties. But not Dr. Michaud—nooooo, he made note of a column by Dave Barry that claimed that Strawberry Pop-Tarts would produce flames if left in a toaster long enough.

Well, it was off to the store to pick up a toaster and some Strawberry Pop-Tarts (SPT as he called them), and thus began the experiment that has now achieved the status of legend.

Patrick started with a toaster, a box of Kellogg's Strawberry Pop-Tarts (with real Smucker's fruit), and a little time on his hands. In careful detail, his Web page recounts the process of setting up the experiment. Of course, an incendiary experiment like this could be dangerous in a normal, enclosed laboratory, so he used the end of his driveway. In went the SPT, on went the Scotch tape, and on went the electricity. Within a few moments, things started to get very interesting.

As he wrote:

At this point the researchers became somewhat concerned that the noise from the toaster would wake the neighbors and attract undue attention. However, we decided that we were already committed to the experiment and that the neighbors would be able to sacrifice some sleep in the name of science.

Soon thereafter, large amounts of smoke began pouring out of the toaster. The researchers noticed that some of the neighbors down the street were beginning to get a little curious, but the experiment proceeded nonetheless. Approximately 40 seconds later, small flames began licking their way out of the toaster. The flames steadily grew larger and larger until reaching a maximum height of about 18 inches above the top of the toaster.

This experiment was quickly ended when the toaster was doused with water.

In retrospect, it's little wonder that Patrick would have explored the outer boundaries of pastries. For gosh sakes, this guy performs radiation experiments on grapes! And his work isn't the only experiment involving Pop-Tarts. That's right—*Patrick is not alone!*

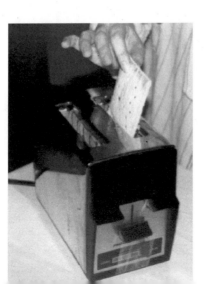

http://www-personal.umich.edu/~gmbrown/tart/

The Flaming Pop-Tart Experiment

Roger A. Hunt, Ph.D. and director of the American Institute of Pyrotartology, apparently also read the very same article written by Dave Barry and decided to try the experiment himself. He got the same results:

1:28:30 Genuinely scary-looking flames shoot from mouths of toaster slots (not unlike those reported by Barry, 1994, p. 65), attaining maximum height of approx. 1.66667 feet. Toaster exterior has begun changing color to an alarming shade of "dark." Observers report seeing curled-up Pop-Tart husks rapidly shriveling inside toaster slots, accompanied by loud crackling noise with occasional sizzles. Lab assistant S. Jones observed coughing as smoke drifts in her direction and complaining about "for better for worse, but nobody mentioned this." Assistant lab assistant Z. Hunt observed yelling to strangers walking dog across the street, "HEY! My dad's burning up our toaster! On purpose!" (Strangers observed accelerating to a trot as they continue across intersection.)

This kind of experiment raises some intriguing possibilities. Considering the kind of explosive results you get from a small tasty pastry, would a larger one yield a bigger result? If you were to create an SPT the size of, say, a semi or a small skyscraper, would you see the same explosive potential as a small nuclear device? And would a few truckloads of regular SPTs achieve the same result?

If this is true, why haven't storage facilities for SPTs been the scene of horrific accidents ("Pop-Tart warehouse in New Jersey detonates, hundreds feared lost")?

Or is there something about the way Pop-Tarts are stored that prevents the possibility of combustion in hotter climates? After all, the inside of buildings in Arizona and New Mexico can reach temperatures similar to the inside of a toaster oven on particularly hot summer days.

And the question also remains: Which experiment came first? Who can lay claim to proving Dave Barry's hypothesis that SPTs can be transformed into incendiary devices?

I originally came across The Strawberry Pop-Tart Blowtorch Page over a year ago.

But, who's to say which was actually first? All that matters is the fact that two different individuals tried this experiment and achieved similar results.

Given that, it's also possible that others will want to perform the same research, but without the safeguards used by these two professionals. In fact, since discovering the second Pop-Tart experiment, I've nervously scanned the newspapers and watched TV news for the tragic story of an amateur who wanted to find out what happens when Pop-Tarts, toasters, and heat are put together.

THE T.W.I.N.K.I.E.S. PROJECT

http://www.owlnet.rice.edu/~gouge/twinkies.html

The long research heritage of the Internet is alive and well and weirder than ever. From the Strawberry Pop Tart Blowtorch experiments to the SpamCam, it's apparent that the Web is a comfortable home to a new breed of aspiring (and bent) Thomas Edisons and Madam Curies. One of the most expansive of these educational sites is the T.W.I.N.K.I.E.S. Project. Now before we go any further, you must realize that "Twinkie" doesn't necessarily refer to the soft, fluffy, cream-filled delicacy that lasts for eons and adds inches to any waistline. On this page, it stands for Tests With Inorganic Noxious Kakes In Extreme Situations. That said, Christopher Gouge and Todd Stadler do their best to put that soft, fluffy, cream-filled delicacy through tests that would make the most jaded laboratory rat nervous.

For example, one test placed a Twinkie under intense radiation (compliments of a microwave oven set on high) for ten minutes. Unfortunately, the test had to be cut off early, for reasons outlined in their test results:

> As soon as the microwave was started, the Twinkie began to ooze creamy filling out onto the bottom of the microwave. After several seconds, the center of the Twinkie collapsed in on itself. The creamy filling bubbled and began to turn brown. Approximately 30 seconds into the test, smoke began to emanate from the interior of the microwave. A strong odor of burned marshmallows began to fill the room.

Soon thereafter the experiment halted as the scientists were overcome by the resulting noxious fumes.

In another fun-filled test, Twinkies were placed in a beaker of water, where they quickly grew to many times their original size, until they began to dissipate into the water. Hmm—it makes me wonder: If the beaker had been large enough, would the Twinkie molecules have become so spread out they could bond with water?

Beyond just presenting their findings, Gouge and Stadler provide inquiries from readers and even rebut some of the more skeptical visitors, as in the following reply to a message:

You said: "Your title suggests that Twinkies are inorganic. Yet most of the major ingredients (oils, sugars, and wheat) are organic. What gives?"

We said: Well, er, uh...sure, they SAY "wheat," but I think in reality they used "Wheet™," the chemically synthesized substitute. Yeah. Plus, I mean, if it looks like a duck, sounds like a duck, it's a duck, right? And Twinkies don't look or sound like ducks, right? And ducks are clearly organic, right? Ipso facto, Twinkies are inorganic. (Please don't rebut about sets and subsets...thank you :) Finally, to conclude, they just don't act organic—sure, organic things may go into Twinkies, but does that mean that they come OUT? Based on our findings, I'd have to say a resounding "No!" with really cool echo effects and stuff like that.

As you wander through this site, you will begin to develop a whole new respect for the lowly Twinkie—and its unique physical properties. A classic example of "edutainment," this Web site can educate the entire family by introducing them to the various physical properties of solid food-like items and showing how to test them using the most delicious of subjects. Now if only someone would explain Vienna sausages...

SpAm CAM

http://www.fright.com/cgi-bin/spamcam

In Cyberspace, food takes on a whole new life, from the frightening experiments involving Strawberry PopTarts and seedless grapes to artistic gems like Meatmation (page 36). Yet, without any doubt, one of the most bizarre, twisted, and just all-around sickest example of fun with food has to be the Spam Cam.

The creation of On&Off Productions, Spam Cam shows in high-resolution detail the effects of time on lowly Spam. How does Spam decompose compared to other organic materials? View the daily decay. Each day is fuzzier, grittier, slimier, and smellier than before. "Visit often," proclaims this smelly site.

And you can keep coming back as the test Spam is reduced back into its base elements— whatever those may be.

Of course, this is a scientific experiment, and in order to give the broadest variety of results, four types of Spam were used:

Regular flavor
SMOKY-FLAVOR
lite
low sodium

Besides the most recent experiment, you'll find images of ongoing ones, as well as contributions from other explorers in the world of decaying food, a massive collection of comments about these experiments, a form to make suggestions on other food you'd like to see run through similar experiments, and links to other equally bizarre food sites on the Web.

interview with **DAWN GROVES**

WWW: Just where did you first come up with the idea for the Spam Cam?

DG: We'd completed work on our first weird site, The Fright Site. Episodic horror. And we were creating an easy doorway to it and thinking about ideas that might appeal to Webbers. Spam—a big Web icon. Cams—also big. Put the two together. A simple fomula for instant acclaim.

WWW: How did your friends react when you began this? Your family?

DG: Our friends think we're nuts. Our family slowly came on board. We'd occasionally see postings in our guestbook from family members. It's a weird experience when your 70-year-old mother calls and says, "So, how's the Spam doing today?"

WWW: I note that you look for suggestions. What's the grossest suggestion you've gotten?

DG: The grossest suggestions are unprintable. We do get a lot of calls for dead bodies, parts of bodies, bodily excretions—use your imagination. Lots of requests for milk products. Roadkill. That sort of thing.

WWW: What kind of e-mail has the Spam Cam generated?

DG: It's amazing how popular the Spam Cam is. And how demanding. We've been rather busy lately and haven't been as attentive as we used to be. The frustrated e-mail we get—it's wild. People demanding updated lab notes. Demanding more close-ups. Wanting Quicktime movies of the decay. Wanting downloadable GIFs.

Whining about how we haven't updated the photo in two days. E-mail is a daunting taskmaster.

We also get lots of supportive e-mail from people who like our humor, who support Mom, apple pie, and rotting Spam. I try to respond to most of the e-mail personally. The kind words are much appreciated. After all, we don't get money for this!

We also receive plenty of political commentary. Lots of rotting politician suggestions from the U.S., U.K., and Canada. I expect an increase in these as the U.S. presidential race heats up.

WWW: Is there any commercial potential? How did the makers of Spam react?
DG: Nah. We don't think there's any commercial potential in this. Part of its appeal is its non-commercial silliness. Mostly, it's a way to attract people to our other sites and

to do something totally off the cuff. If we started making money, Spam Inc. [actually, Hormel] would probably want a piece of the action. As it is, they haven't contacted us one way or the other. We hope they have a sense of humor and that they leave us alone.

WWW: What kind of results have you found that were interesting? Any suprises?
DG: I think the moldy Twinkie was a surprise. No one believes that Twinkies rot. And when we tried to rot Cheese Whiz, it NEVER changed. Even now, it's sitting outside in the elements, still as orange and smooth as the day it was spread "two months ago." Now THAT'S a result!

A month ago when I was photographing an experiment that included a marshmallow Peep (you know, those dorky marshmallow critters that grace Easter baskets), I inadvertently pushed the Peep out of the way, snapped the photo, and uploaded it. The thunderstorm of e-mail I received the next day was staggering. Where's the Peep? What happened to the Peep? The Peep is gone! Did it run away? Is it dead?

This lead to an exploding-Peep episode of the Spam Cam that I'm still sorting out. We brought the Peeps back en masse. People kept writing about them. It was legendary silliness.

When someone comes to our home, it's amusing to observe visitor responses to the 'lab area' (also known as the dining room). People see plates of truly disgusting-looking food remnants and just…sort of…walk…in the other…direction. No comment. Not a word.

Even stranger, people think that we must be young, wild, college students. In fact, we're gainfully employed, middle class, perfectly ordinary thirty-something people—who run the hottest rotting food cam on the Web!

WWW: What's next? Any other food groups you'd like to explore?
DG: We're looking at other kinds of canned meat products. Perhaps different brands. Even other nationalities. U.S. Spam versus Australian Vegemite versus Canadian potted meat. We'll put up little flags, maybe include sound files of national anthems and so on. Perhaps an Olympic Rot-a-Thon. We're also going to do some comparisons of combination fast foods, such as Big Macs, Whoppers, and pizza.

Naturally, a Spam loaf will be also present in each of these experiments, as a control.

We'd like to add other rotting food cams, perhaps automate

them so we're not lab-bound. And we keep asking for visitors to send us photos of their moldy food to add to our Homegrown section. We expected a stronger response than we've gotten so far. I guess people prefer watching food rot in someone ELSE's home. Oh, well.

WWW: What kind of advice would you have for anyone doing their own weird site? Or experiments with food products?
DG: Food product experiments are a major challenge. People CARE about them. (Go figure!) Of course, the result is that you get thousands of people who care about your rotting food but who don't have to live with it. I'd advise food product experimenters to understand the seriousness of the endeavor. Once you engage a loyal audience of food-decay enthusiasts, you're stuck with maintaining piles of moldy garbage around

the house for months at a time. Lovely.

It also twists your mind. Now, every time I see old food in the fridge or look into a trashcan full of used food bags, I think SPAM CAM! Moldy food is a force of nature. It's no longer something to be thrown out. It's something to be photographed, studied, cherished.

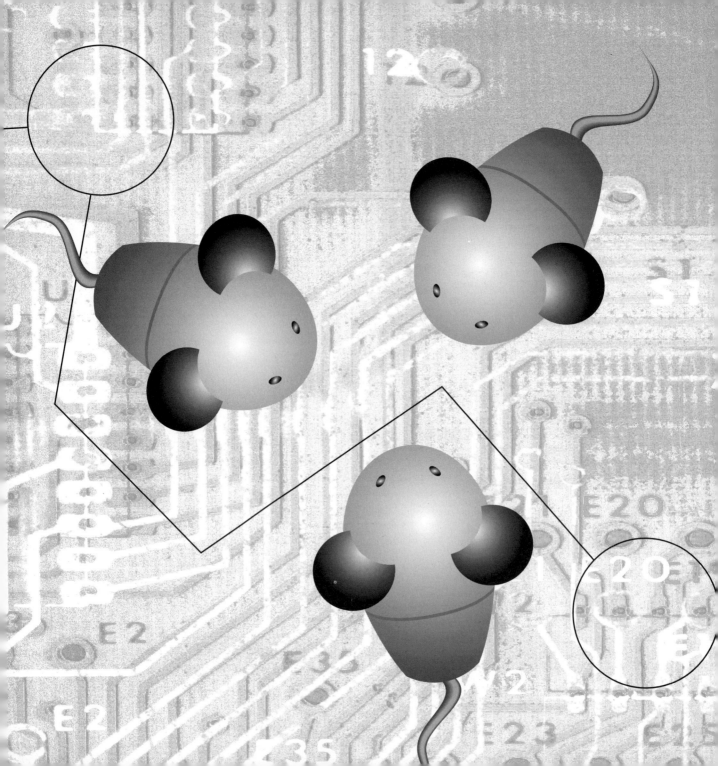

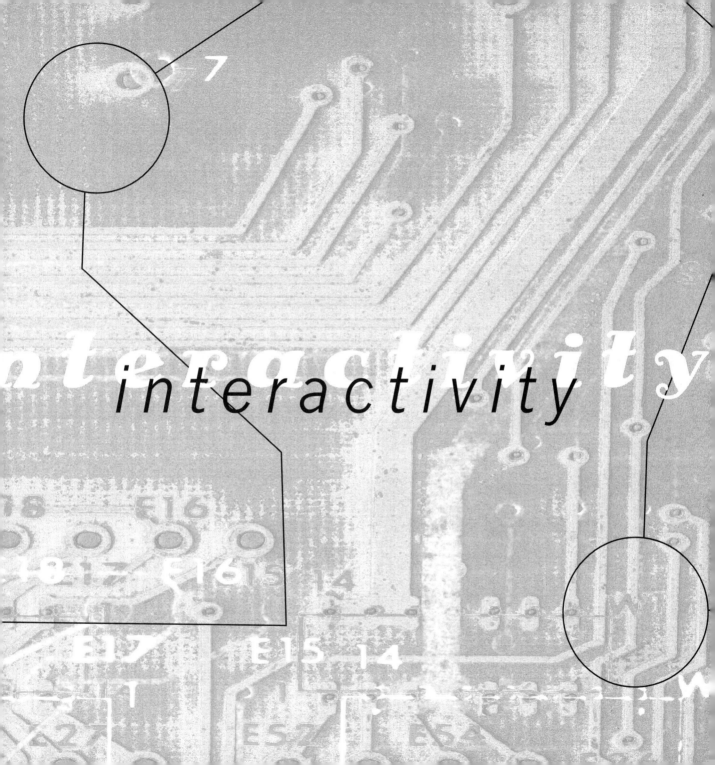

interactivity

get your

ASS KICKED

on the web

http://www.hypno.com/ass/ass.html

Have you ever wondered what it would be like to head to the other side of town? You know—across the tracks? You'd search out the roughest-looking dive—the one that has a passel of Harleys...and *more* than one ambulance parked in front—apparently just waiting for something to happen. You'd stroll in the front door, let the bartender know that you want to make an announcement, and in your wimpiest voice, announce, "I just backed my car over seven of those butt-ugly bikes out front, and I wanted to let you know that *I enjoyed every second of it!*" Then close your eyes and wait for the fun to begin.

If you have...YOU ARE ONE SICK PUPPY! And you need to visit Get Your Ass Kicked on the World Wide Web!

This page is designed for the violence-loving masochist. Once you arrive, you've got your choice of two characters (the She-Devil and the Crusher) to assist you in this act of extreme self-abuse. They will gladly beat, bend, twist, and mutilate you.

the she-devil

the crusher

OK, OK—to be honest, this site doesn't do any physical harm to your persona—only to a convenient photograph. You take the image you wish

to let either of these questionable characters have their way with and send it to them as an e-mail using the Kick My Ass button. A short time later, the image will return, suitably mutilated and ravaged.

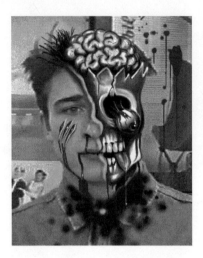

Sound like fun? Well, there is no rule that the image you send them has to be *yours*! Got a boss that's a little too huffy? Let the Crusher have his way with 'em. A young one who's sowing too damn many wild oats? The She-Devil will definitely sow AND HARVEST the ungrateful ankle-biter!

Get Your Ass Kicked can be fun for the whole family. Of course, that family must be a seriously twisted one.

interview with **GREG THATCHER**

WWW: What's the story behind this site?
GT: We wanted a forum for our artists' creativity. Creators included Dana Muise (artist), James Mattly (programmer), Andy Karn (programmer), and other artists. We wanted to try out new technologies like Java and Shockwave. To develop new Internet apps. To make our page better than all of our friends' pages.

WWW: How much effort was it?
GT: We've been working on it for a year and a half.

WWW: Where and how do you gather your content?
GT: A programmer wants to try a new technology, or an artist makes some new art, or one of us gets drunk and starts typing HTML code.

WWW: What kind of reaction did your friends and relatives have to this site?
GT: My friends liked it a lot. My mother should have been disappointed, but she *loved* it.

WWW: The local police?
GT: We keep moving so they can't find us.

WWW: What's next?
GT: Probably some really sick Shockwave demos. We're also working on a couple of Internet multiplayer games that will be hosted on our site.

WWW: Have you learned any lessons from doing something this bizarre?
GT: Some people don't have a sense of humor. We currently making another site (www.hypno.net) so that our few politically correct customers will have something to look at.

WWW: Any advise for other Web publishers?
GT: Do some research before picking an ISP. We had to move our Web site a bunch of times because the ISP was too slow or because we got too many hits and they wanted to charge us exorbitant amounts of money. In the end, we had to buy our own dedicated ISDN line to handle the traffic.

WWW: What of person would you like to attract to a site like this?
GT: Someone who thinks most of the Web is boring. Someone who wants to see what programmers and artists can do when they aren't shackled by a corporate culture.

OVI'S WORLD OF THE BIZARRE

http://netmar.com/users/ovigher/ovi.htm

I firmly believe that truth is weirder than fiction. Maybe that's why I get such a sick kind of kick out of reading the most out-there supermarket tabloids, was a big-time fan of Real People, and secretly love to watch Geraldo.

Ovi's a lot like this as well. His World of the Bizarre Web site has a truly twisted selection of reality-based stories. Scanning through a recent issue, I discovered stories about a man who took a radio station hostage in order hear a Kermit the Frog song, a woman who attempted to castrate her husband, a camel who returned to its owner after 4 years, and a 1-inch cockroach that was pulled out of a Swedish tourist's ear.

Some of the stories are funny, some are horrifying, and some are just plain weird, but they're always changing and always unpredictable.

interview with **OVI**

WWW: What was your inspiration for this site?
OVI: As a semi-disgruntled postal worker, I felt that nothing seemed more appropriate (and natural) than a bizarre-subject Web page. Actually, I had a reputation among my (small) group of friends for collecting bizarre-but-true news reports. When the Web exploded as a new publishing medium for weird people like myself, I jumped on the opportunity to offer the cyberspace community something valuable, entertaining, and interesting. The Web allows "average" people to express themselves in any way they want. I believe that there is something weird in all of us.

WWW: Where and how do you select your content?
OVI: I refrain from printing every weird story I get my hands on. Because I am an information junkie, most of my stories come from local publications, and some over the newswire.

I use a very selective process, which I call the S.A.D. approach. I rely on the help of my beautiful girlfriend, Shon Hogans—my number-one fan, supporter, and consultant—to hand-pick my stories. I ask Shon to read the stories out loud and I watch her reactions. Here is how the S.A.D. approach works:

Shocking = *It must make a sudden impact on the reader (good or bad). This is the step where I listen for remarks such as "Wow!" "Say what?!" and so on.*

ovi's world of the bizarre

Amazing = *It must strike the reader as an unusual (unheard-of) type of story. Here I listen for statements such as "Is this true?"*

Disbelief = *The reader's judgment and emotions are activated. This is where the reader either accepts the story or tries to find logical explanations. Usually this is followed by: "Where are you getting this stuff from?"*

If Shon reacts according to the S.A.D. principle, then that particular story is worthy of display on Ovi's World of the Bizarre.

I sometimes refer to my page as "my baaaaaby." I have declined a couple of offers from people interested in acquiring me and my page. I believe that would kill the freedom of creativity and expression. (Not only that, but my $1 million asking price seemed to turn them off for some reason.)

WWW: How much effort does the page require?
OVI: Creating a bizarre (weird) page is a continuous effort. Above all, it must be a hobby, and frequent updates must be provided.

WWW: What kind of reaction did your friends have to the site?
OVI: Although my friends refrained from making direct comments (who would? I'm "the bizarre guy," after all), the Web community reaction was overwhelmingly positive. I now have thousands of loyal fans across the world, most of them addicts to the strange-but-true subject. Overall, 99% of all the comments I received have been positive and encouraging. Surprisingly, 60% of my viewers come from large corporations.

WWW: How do you feel now that it's up?
OVI: Because of my desire to publish a bizarre page, I have the satisfaction of doing something I enjoy. Plus, I get to keep up with HTML, CGI, and the fast-changing Web-authoring field.

WWW: What's next?
OVI: Other than continuing to provide frequent updates, I would like to raise the level of interactivity with my users. The page is getting a facelift in the next few weeks (the original will still be available). Other projects (all of which will be available by the time this book is published) will include:

A search engine for the growing archive

A poll script/user voting

A random story feature

An e-mail subscription featuring the best stories of the week

A contest (small prizes)

The best of the bizarre — a "Top 20"

WWW: What words of wisdom can you offer other potential Web publishers?
OVI:

* Let your creativity flow.

* Don't be offensive to one, or any, particular group. (Entertainment to ALL is the key.)

* Beware of copyright laws.

* Once it's created, update your page as frequently as possible.

* Add a link in your page to Ovi's World of the Bizarre.

* REMEMBER: BIZARRE IS GOOD!!

http://www.streams.com/pierce/index.html

Have you ever wandered through a really cool neighborhood and felt envious of all the hip slackers wandering aimlessly? No, I'm not talking about wishing you could spend your days nursing a latte and your nights explaining to your parents why you can't move out just yet. Or wanting to wear baggy pants that didn't show your butt so that you looked like a "gangsta" instead of a "plumba." Or even that you were 20-something, and not, ahhh, er, something else!

No, I'm talking about the world of body modification. In truly with-it areas, you'll see tons of tattoos, enough brands to make a steer nervous, and people who look like they fell face first into a tackle box.

I have felt this envy many times but, like so many wimps, I just can't get into the pain side of it. I mean, I've spent months looking for clip-on nose rings and believable stick-on tattoos.

Finally, I found salvation on the Web through Piercing Mildred, a site that would satisfy the most sadistic body modifier. Here, you start by picking a character to have your way with. You have your choice of Mitch, Maurice, or, of course, Mildred. You start with $100, a nekkid subject, and the commands pierce, scar, mutilate (just kidding), heal. Click "pierce" and you'll be presented with a choice of body locations to pierce and the price for each; click "scar" and you're charged for the size of scar you want. And "heal" is only used when one of your piercings/scars becomes infected. God, is this real or what?

Every week there's a contest for the most unusual body modifications. Win and you become one of the Freaks of the Week!

Bear in mind that there are some seriously twisted entries on a given week, so you may have to push the boundaries of good taste to be a winner. Whatever happens, the best thing about Piercing Mildred is that you can try any kind of body mod that you might dream about, and when you're finished, not only are you not sore at all (unless you get really physical with your mouse!), but if you don't like the results, you just quit the program.

 interview with **DAVE SKWARCZEK**

WWW: What drove you to create this site?
DS: Well, we live in the heart of Chicago's artist community; supposedly there are more artists per capita here than anywhere in the world. As a result, everyone here has pierced EVERYTHING. It's trendy to at least have a Prince Albert.

And we were into the Net, which we figured was going to completely explode like it has. So, we combined the nineties' two favorite pastimes: body modification and the Internet.

WWW: Were there any accomplices?
DS: Everyone here at Streams, the online design firm I work with, paid their dues to Mme. Mildred.

WWW: How much effort was this page?
DS: About 400 hours of work to put it together, plus another few hours a week

since then for care and feeding.

WWW: Where and how do you gather your content?
DS: Our brains! We are usually inspired by whatever's around us —whatever the press is yapping about, things we see in our neighborhood, and so on. Our brains sort of act as little environmental blenders.

WWW: What kind of reaction did your friends have to this site?
DS: They all thought the idea was an original one. Then they asked me what the Internet was.

WWW: Your relatives?
DS: My parents didn't understand this whole Internet thing until they started hearing about it everywhere! Then they started getting into it. Now they want me to help 'em buy a new computer, get them set up on-

line, etc. Those crazy kids.

WWW: *The local police?*
DS: Actually, we got an anonymous call from some joker who said he'd called the Chicago police and the FBI about one of our other satirical Web-zines, *Brian*, because we did a pretty harsh restaurant review that was inspired by all the hoopla in the press about militias and the Unabomber. People sometimes miss the completely obvious — like the fact that *Brian* magazine as a whole is obviously a satirical rant.

He wouldn't tell me who he was. Then he hung up. This man probably also wears a belt and suspenders simultaneously.

WWW: *How has the Web-wandering community reacted to it?*
DS: Pretty well. We're currently getting about 1,500 people playing Piercing Mildred every day. There are around 4,500 active characters.

WWW: *What's next?*
DS: Auto-logon features; tattooing; VRMiLdred, where you'll be able to pierce your character in 3-D (for example, through the head) as well as fly inside to pierce and tattoo internal organs.

The most recent work we did was for the Subway Web Site. It's at http://www.subway.com/. My favorite part of the site is a Shockwave game called the Amazing Virtual Subway. The basic concept is that you have to build a sub and eat as many

of them as you can before your soda runs out. It's really funny. Terry Gilliam's brilliant animation was definitely an inspiration.

We are currently working on other online pieces like Brian (streams.com/brian), Planet Starchild (streams.com/starchild), and Litweb (streams.com/litweb). We're also developing some new networked online games that are going to be really groovy.

But developing corporate Web sites is what pays the bills around here.

WWW: Have you learned any lessons from doing something this bizarre?
DS: People are weirder than I ever thought possible. Our fan mail is truly odd.

WWW: What advice do you have for other Web wannabes?
DS: Go with it.

WWW: What kind of person would you like to attract to a site like this?
DS: We hope we're reaching intelligent people with a very keen wit. Or total morons.

WWW: What are your goals?
DS: To get some sleep.

WWW: How do you feel now that it's up?
DS: Pierced.

OBSES
obsessions
SIONS

THE ANGRY

What makes you angry? I don't mean "mildly irritated"—I mean, hurl the baseball bat at the TV, throw the VCR out the window, cut off your boss's tie, drop a hydrogen bomb on the bus that left you standing there angry! Or, as one of my favorite columnists, Ed Anger of the *Weekly World News*, would say—PIG BITING MAD!

If you'd like to share that anger with the rest of the World point your browser at "The Crankiest Site on the Net," as The Angry Organization's home page proclaims itself. Here are collected lists of companies, organizations, people, and things that make us angry. As the creator, AngryMan, says, "I am truly amazed at the amount of anger out there in the world. The Angry Organization is based on your anger, your angst and your fire."

The range of anger expressed here varies from the frustrated to the seriously pissed off. Each visitor can read through people's tirades on every subject imaginable, from the obvious

> *The Post Office Why do the lazy bastards advertise? They are not in competition with anybody. If private companies were allowed to deliver the mail, the Post Orifice would be out of business. They don't allow competition! The only thing postal employees do well is shoot one another.*

http://www.angry.org

...to the surprising

*The Arbor Day Association I thought I would do a good deed and donate
$15.00 to the Arbor Day Foundation as requested, in order to receive a mem-
bership with their organization. With your membership, they promise you ten
FREE trees (I was looking forward to my new trees!) and they send you a little
catalog with all kinds of trees for you to pick out. At the end of each little
paragraph describing each tree, it lists states they cannot ship to. Not once
under any of those paragraphs does it say, "Cannot ship to California," which
is where I live—that is, until you get to the very last page of their catalog
where, in small print, it says they cannot ship ANY trees into the state of
California and miscellaneous other states also listed!*

...to the downright obscure

*Donald Duck Abusers Hey, have you noticed that every time Donald Duck
tries to catch those damn rats, or whatever the hell they are, he ends up getting hurt himself? It makes me pretty damn upset to see those stupid rodents
being ignorant of other people's feelings. All they care about is their damn
tree, and nuts, and that useless crap. Why don't they let Donald win sometimes? What's there to lose?*

Page after page of anger spouting from minds, fingers, and keyboards all over
the world. And when you're angry enough, you can add your own entry.

So don't just get angry, point your browser toward The Angry Page, and get
angry along with the rest of us!!

ORGANIZATION

WWW: What drove you to create this site?

JM: I was sitting telling a couple of friends and co-workers about how I'd get angry at people who sent e-mail with dumb questions or comments when I used to run a couple of bulletin board systems here in San Francisco. I was also telling them about how I got kicked off a couple of systems for name-calling and ad hominem attacks. We thought it would be cool to have a place that we could just bitch and moan at people. After scraping up a machine, I created Angry.Org.

WWW: Were there any accomplices?

JM: My boss, Robert Faludi, was a huge help. We both thought Angry.Org would be just a neat little toy to play with. We had no idea we would be getting 100,000 hits a day!

WWW: What are your goals?

JM: To have the site evolve to encompass everything and everyone we should be angry about. I hope that, by seeing everything that angers people around the world, we can agree that some things really deserve some rage.

WWW: How much effort was this page?

JM: Initially, the page was nothing. The graphics were horrible but you could click a "mail-to:" link on the site to send in your anger. The graphics still suck today, but now, because of the volume of e-mail I get, I've automated the submission process. I spend a lot of time sifting through the anger of people all over the world. I really cannot believe how specific people get with things that tick them off.

WWW: Where and how do you gather your content?

JM: That is the best part. The anger comes to me in a nice little package of HTML. I have a form set up to assist both the angry person and my cataloging efforts. When people want to add their anger, they can fill-out an online form that automatically sends a customized HTML page to me via e-mail. So I get formatted HTML pages about yeast infection commercials, the prime meridian, roommates who pick their noses, and many, many, many other bizarre people, companies, organizations, and things that seem to generate anger in the minds of people all over the globe.

WWW: What reaction did your friends have when first told them about it? Your relatives?

JM: They were all very supportive. My sister and brother thought that it was hilarious. Some of my friends wondered why the hell I would spend time absorbing anger and putting it on display, but they got over it after they saw how damn funny the site was.

WWW: The local police?

JM: No calls yet. As a matter of fact, that makes me kind of angry.

WWW: How has the Web-wandering community reacted to it?

JM: I am truly amazed we have been able to hit such a nerve with people worldwide. Only the Internet would have allowed us the ability to put out this type of angry data and have people say, "Wow, yeah, that ticks me off too!" in a few different languages.

WWW: How do you feel now that it's up?

JM: I actually felt better when it was just a little tiny entity: It was so manageable and easy. I mean, I am honored that people really find it to be a great site to browse, but I feel very overwhelmed now—because every time I go to check my e-mail, I have like 500 messages to sift through every day. Sometimes I feel like I have created a monster I cannot control, sometimes I feel like it is my own damn fault for being overwhelmed. Then, I start to get angry again.

WWW: What's next?

JM: I think Angry.Org will start spawning. Perhaps "politics.angry.org" or something. I don't really know. I know we need better artwork. My artwork sucks.
I think I'll start looking at sponsors (Prozac maybe?).
I think we can really keep this ball rolling, because we have so much support from so many people— I can't let them down. We can only get angrier.

WWW: Have you learned any lessons from doing something this bizarre?

JM: Be careful what you wish for—the Internet probably can deliver it.

WWW: What words of wisdom can you offer other potential Web publishers?

JM: Find out what interests you and what you feel is missing on the Internet, then pervert and exploit it. Voilá—a weird and twisted Web site that everyone wants to take a look at.

WWW: What kind of person would you like to attract to your site?

JM: People who know how bizarre the real world is will be attracted to this site because we are the reflection of the negative energy of the world. We dip so deep in the anger that we actually bring you full circle and make you laugh, because there are so many articles that everyone can identify with.

The Interactive Ego Booster

http://web.syr.edu/~ablampac/ego/index.html

Do you ever have one of those days when you just don't want to get out of bed?

No, I'm not talking about when you'd rather luxuriate in the soft embrace of warm blankets on a cold morning, or even when you'd rather not go to work/school/whatever. I'm speaking of those days when you just think, "Why bother? I mean, it doesn't really matter." We've all had times when our egos are in ebb, and we honestly don't think anything is going to work out.

Take heart, depressed souls. Now there's the Interactive Ego Booster! Yes, the World Wide Web has become home to one of the best tonics for the "feeling-down syndrome" since a smile and wink from a cute co-worker (which of course, in these days of sexual harassment, can be more dangerous than helpful).

Click! and the page returns "Everybody should be more like you!"

Wait a moment, and it'll decide that "You are very, very, very special."

A bit longer and "When they made you, they broke the mold."

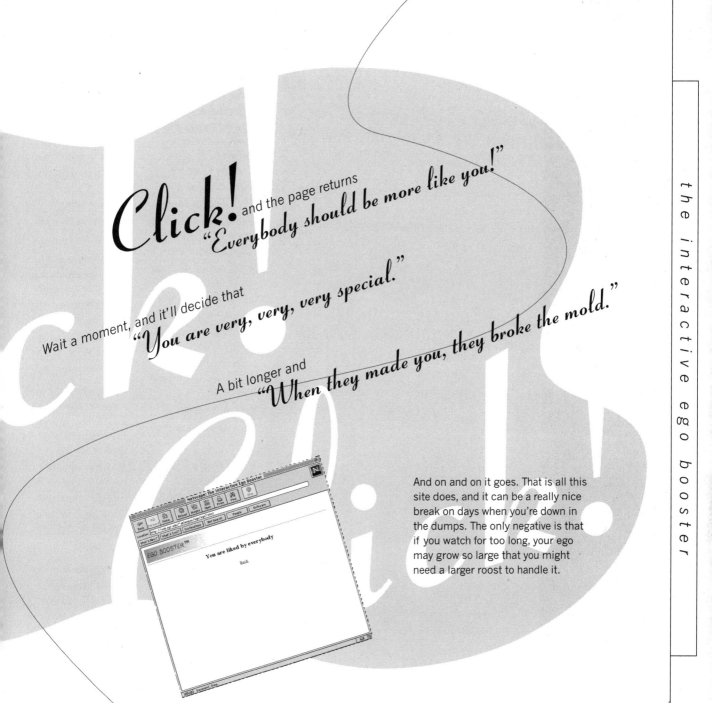

Netscape: The Interactive Ego Booster

EGO BOOSTER™

You are liked by everybody

Back

And on and on it goes. That is all this site does, and it can be a really nice break on days when you're down in the dumps. The only negative is that if you watch for too long, your ego may grow so large that you might need a larger roost to handle it.

WWW: What was your inspiration or, maybe more accurately, what drove you to create this site?

AL: Many years ago when my friend got his first computer (a Mac), it had a microphone to record sounds. One of the things we did was record ourselves telling ourselves how great we were. These were supposed to boost our egos. When I was trying to think of original content for my Web page, I thought it would be funny to do the same thing.

WWW: What are your goals?

AL: I hope people come to The Interactive Ego Booster and get a laugh out of it. I see a lot of Web stuff out there and hope I can add my two cents to the pot.

WWW: How much effort did it take to create this page?

AL: Creating the page wasn't very difficult. Coming up with the idea took a while. It's not easy being weird—it only looks that way.

WWW: Where and how do you go about gathering your content?

AL: Content was easy. I tried to produce the cheesiest-sounding inspirational sayings you might ever hear.

WWW: What kind of reaction did your friends have to this site when you first told them about it?

AL: Most told me I have way too much time on my hands. The other ones said, "What's the World Wide Web??"

WWW: Your relatives?

AL: My mom was proud. My dad thought this was a result of a poor upbringing.

WWW: The local police?
AL: My lawyer has advised me not to comment on the police's reaction until after the trial (kidding).

WWW: How has the Web-wandering community reacted to it?
AL: I've gotten many responses. Most people tell me what a great idea it is and that they check it every day to get them started in the morning. Some people still tell me I have too much free time.

WWW: How do you feel now that it's up?
AL: I feel pretty good about it.

WWW: What's next??
AL: I have The Ego Booster in English and Dutch. I hope to expand it to other languages as well. I'm trying to concoct some new and interesting sites for people to see. Creating bizarre ideas is tough. It's mentally straining.

WWW: Have you learned any lessons from doing something this bizarre?
AL: There are weird people out there who appreciate the bizarre. It's very frightening.

WWW: What kind of words of wisdom can you give other lost souls who have this itch they just gotta scratch to put out a truly weird Web wonder?
AL: The crazier you think you are for doing it, the better the page will be.

WWW: What kind of person would you like to attract to a site like this?
AL: Anyone who has some time to waste and doesn't mind stupidity.

You suck up to Nazis, you anal retentive, barf

ABUSE ME AGAIN!

ABUSE ME AGAIN!

ABUSE ME AGAIN!

ABUSE ME AGAIN!

E ME AGAIN!

ABUSE ME AGAIN!

ABUSE ME AGAIN!

slime mold of a saliva-

ABUSE ME AGAIN!

ABUSE ME AGAIN!

USE ME AGAIN!

vert.

ABUSE-A-TRON

Have you ever had times when you feel too good? That's right. You're in an excruciatingly cheery mood, everything seems perfect with the world, and you begin to get the sinking feeling that either all this will end suddenly and horribly, or your friends will desert you because they're tired of you being so damned HAPPY!

It's times like these when Abuse-A-Tron comes in handy. It's pretty straight ahead. Once you arrive, you merely select a button that reads **HEAP ABUSE UPON US** and Abuse-A-Tron will return something natty like

"*You suck up to Nazis, you anal retentive, barf-gargling, mutant turtle-feeling, plasmoidal slime mold of a salivation-empowered pervert.*"

Still feeling painfully pleasant? Just click

and you might learn that

"*You carry pieces of garbage in your pockets for ID, you drooling, pus-gulping, elephant-feeling, vacillating begetter of an incestuous politician.*"

And on and on it goes, until you either click the

STOP! STOP! AAARGH! button,

or you take your own life (or someone else's).

interview with ED BEBEE

WWW: What was your inspiration or, more accurately, what drove you to create this site?
EB: I was asked by CPC Loyalty Communications (my then-employer) to create a Web site that would generate a lot of traffic, but it didn't have to be commercial. I wanted something with a unique hook, and the idea of spewing abuse at people seemed appealing. Also, the Jerky Boys were popular at the time so I was able to dupe—I mean, convince other people at CPC that this idea would fly.

WWW: Were there any accomplices, or are you the only one that can be held liable?
EB: If there's a jail sentence involved, I'm not going alone. There were a handful of others involved. At CPC, there was Heather Payne, who helped with proofing the insults (she took out the really provocative stuff), databasing the results of the site, going through the mail, and so on. This huge job was later taken over by George Alletson. The CGI script and a lot of tech support were developed by Steve Dengler, Ed Faddies, and Beric Farmer at Xenon Laboratories, on whose server the Abuse-A-Tron rests.

WWW: How much effort did it take to create this page?
EB: The actual assembly was easy. Writing the original insults and putting together a random sentence that would be grammatically correct most of the time took a few days.

WWW: Where and how did you gather your content?
EB: I sat at the back of a divorce court and took notes. Ha!

Actually, I sat down with a dictionary and a thesaurus for two or three afternoons and wrote stuff out as I found words I liked. Once the site was up, visitors to it started supplying content.

WWW: How did your friends react to your site when you first told them about it?
EB: They would call me up and repeat abuse that they read off the site at me in high-pitched, fake British voices.

Most of them thought it was cool. A few thought it was weird. My immediate boss told me we weren't going to do it because it was offensive and he didn't want to piss people off. My mom thought it was typical of me.

WWW: How has the Web-wandering community reacted to it?
EB: Fairly well. The site was flooded with people when it first opened. I haven't kept up with it, but it receives an average of fifteen letters a day. Most are positive.

WWW: What's next?
EB: The Abuse-A-Tron has been in limbo for a while since I left CPC to work elsewhere. Recently, I've negotiated with CPC and gotten the rights to the Web site, so I have a few changes planned, including a facelift and expansion of the code behind it so that it will do a greater variety of things—but I'm not telling what just yet!

WWW: Have you learned any lessons from doing something this bizarre?
EB: People are much weirder than I suspected.

Don't compromise or you get compromised.

WWW: What kind of words of wisdom would you give other lost souls who have this itch they just gotta scratch to put up a truly weird Web wonder?
EB: DO IT! PUBLISH SOMETHING! The WWW is currently like a billion-channel TV—it needs *good* content. People need something weird to activate their minds.

Besides, even if the absolute worst happens and everything goes wrong, you can always change your name and leave the country.

WWW: What kind of person would you like to attract to a site like this?
EB: Anyone with a sense of humor and a bit of time to write a comment back to me. I'm always interested in what people think.

WWW: What are your long-term goals?
EB: To sell out and make truckloads of cash from some huge pig of a company.

WWW: How do you feel now that your site is up?
EB: Great! The treatments the doctor gave me never did #$%@ but in the past few minutes...Sorry, were you referring to the Web site?

I feel really good. Every once in a while I get bit of recognition or find out that people are using it in their workplace to break up the monotony, so there's a positive side to all this abuse.

I sometimes feel sad that I was born into a generation that came of age in the heart of the decadent 70s. Instead of relevant discussions about serious issues, we worried about how to get our mood rings to turn blue again. No aggressive gangsta rap or grunge rock for us; we were invited to "Shake shake shake; Shake shake shake; Shake your booty." Anyway, we were deprived of our inalienable right to feel awful.

If you, too, find yourself looking longingly at a group of 20-something slackers slurping down decaf double lattes (with a twist, of course) in dreary coffee shops while listening to depressing post-beat poetry, then Ask Mr. Angst is for you!

Jim Fieser has enough attitude to fill the Superdome, and he unleashes it all on this paean to modern culture.

Just how much angst does he have? Check This Out:

http://unix1.utm.edu/~jfieser/angst.htm

Dear Mr. Angst:

Today I picked a flower. Its texture was hope, its colors were tranquility and beatitude, and its fragrance was love. Just thought you's like to know.
Signed, Inner Child

Dear Inner Child: That was very touchy feely of you. I too picked a flower today. It reminded me that for each flower we heed, acres of less-appreciated plants are mowed down, yanked out by their roots, or slashed and burned. Its perfection spoke of the other flowers of its species that are rejected because their stems are too long, their colors less vibrant, or their petals open un-symmetrically. Its alluring smell serves to manipulate insects to perform the dance of cross-pollination on its behalf. And look how we use the flower's exploitative force for our own purposes. I cannot win you over on my own merits, so I distract you with this flower while I have my way!

Your loved one dies. What is that to me? I present to you this flower arrangement to veil my own indifference. It seems, Inner Child, that we have a shared appreciation for the flower and that which it evokes.

As you can see, Mr. Angst lives up to his name, spouting enough cut-to-the-chase, reality-based rhetoric to depress Barney the Dinosaur. Yet, somewhere in all this negative space are some real gems of humor and insight (enough to make even me feel cool).

WWW: What drove you to create this site?
JF: It started out as a column for a college paper at a school where I was teaching. Originally it was called Ask Mr. Philosophy, and I later changed it to Ask Mr. Angst. That was about 10 years ago. I had the old articles on disk. Last year I decided to spruce up my personal Web page with original writing. I HTML-ized a few of the articles, put a "Submit Question" mail-to button on the page, and, presto! the Ask Mr. Angst Web site was born.

WWW: Were there any accomplices?
JF: David Sofranko, the editor of the school newspaper in which the first column appeared, tossed in ideas for the very first column. He has since gotten a Masters in journalism, married a Swedish girl, and moved to London.

WWW: What are your goals?
JF: The goal of the column is to make people laugh, vent my own frustrations, and explore atypical perspectives on reality.

WWW: How much effort goes into this page?
JF: Unfortunately, when I'm actively updating the page, it is a tremendous effort. I get about one inquiry a day. Three-quarters of the questions are unusable. Some are as strange as the answers I try to give in response. It is a difficult task to be continually funny and creative, so each response takes almost an hour to write and fine-tune.

WWW: Where and how do you gather your content?
JF: Some questions naturally generate their own answers.

The contents of others are the results of wacky ideas I've knocked around for a while.

WWW: What kind of reaction did your friends and relatives have to this site?
JF: Friends, and especially students, who see the site are initially a bit surprised that I produced it, but are very flattering. My mother is, of course, so proud of me. A free-lance writer, she helped edit several of the early newspaper columns for me.

WWW: The local police?
JF: I have a love/hate relationship with the police. As long as they protect me from the bad guys, then I love them. Otherwise…

WWW: How has the Web-wandering community reacted to it?
JF: Some replies have been very ego-boosting. The editor of the magazine *Internet Underground* saw the article and wrote blurbs on it for two of

their issues. Other replies are very insulting. For example, here's one from the other day: What the hell is the point of this stupid page? Just how many people do you think read this? I think your page is a crock of @#$%!"

WWW: How do you feel now that it's up?
JF: I feel both burdened by its upkeep yet satisfied that I am contributing to the decline of civilization.

WWW: What's next?
JF: When I have the time, I'd like to post more of the short stories I've written, which are just as bizarre as Ask Mr. Angst.

WWW: Have you learned any lessons from creating this site?
JF: From my perspective, the more I add to the page, the less bizarre it seems to me—although to the browser it remains pretty strange.

WWW: What words of wisdom would you give other lost souls who want to create a weird Web wonder?
JF: Find an interest, get creative, then consciously push your creativity one step further to make something unique. Don't rely on cheap laughs (such as dirty words) to be entertaining.

WWW: What sort of person would you like to attract to your site?
JF: Anyone who wouldn't classify themselves as a "born-again Christian."

Ask Mr. BadAdvice

http://www.echonyc.com/~spingo/Mr.BA/

You can find a lot of things on the World Wide Web: a lot of information about companies and their products; a lot of pictures of interesting things; a lot of forms that you can fill out; and a lot of advice.

And among the advice-related pages out there, none is worse than this one. Ask him any kind of question on any kind of topic, and he'll respond to it—sometimes humorously, sometimes bizarrely, sometimes avoiding the topic entirely—but always badly.

You can always count on Mr. Bad Advice to tell you exactly what you didn't need to know.

What kind of bad advice has Mr. Bad Advice given out?

Now, you may wonder, why in the heck would you go to the trouble of getting an Internet connection, struggling with its configuration, and then spending hours searching around the Net to find Mr. Bad Advice—just to get some lame answer to your serious question?

Well, to be honest, I don't really know, and anything I'd tell you would be bad advice.

Dear Mr. Bad Advice,
My company just laid me off, and I have two weeks until I face unemployment. My car is a #%&*&# 1978 Pacer, and I just got a date with this really hot girl that I met at the Bowl-A-Rama. Trouble is, she's a mechanic. What should I do with my last $350?
Signed, Poor and Horny
Dear Anxious,
Is she cute?

Dear Mr. Bad Advice,
During yesterday's jujitsu class, I hurt the little toe on my right foot in a bad landing breakfall. It didn't seem too bad at the time, but this morning when I tried to walk on my foot, it hurt a lot. Should I go see a doctor about this, or wait a few more days to see if it heals naturally?
Regards, John
Dear John,
That's kind of a boring name, isn't it?

Dear Mr. Bad Advice,
Should I go see some guys play softball on Sunday or will they be so lame that it'd be better to watch ants cross a piece of concrete?
Dear Sports Fan,
Ants have many more legs, for what it's worth.

interview with **JAMES BARNETT**

WWW: What drove you to create this site?
JB: An off-the-cuff comment from my girlfriend, Molly Ker, general manager of Echo, when we were both on Echo one night—"You know, you really are Mr. Bad Advice"—after I'd suggested some ridiculous solution to a problem. (Echo's a conferencing system in NYC—telnet echonyc.com.)

WWW: Were there any accomplices?
JB: Molly had the idea, Josh Masur did the logo, and various pals sent me my first batch of questions.

WWW: What are your goals?
JB: To make people laugh and get a little bit of recognition, both of which I've achieved—I was voted a CyberStar by *Virtual City* mag and was reviewed favorably in *Entertainment Weekly* and *Wired*.

WWW: How much effort does this page need?
JB: Not all that much. At this point the questions that come in (several a day, even after a year) are better than I could ever expect, so the answering is easy.

WWW: Where and how do you gather your content?
JB: All of the questions are reprinted verbatim and not written by me. I get a couple a day. I just answer 'em, put 'em in a table template, and there ya go.

WWW: What kind of reaction did your friends and relatives have to the site?
JB: They all dug it.

WWW: The local police?
JB: Uh, I don't know if they know about it yet, but my pal John the Cop does.

WWW: Have you learned any lessons from doing something this bizarre?
JB: People are weirder than I thought. I was in no way prepared for the quality of letters I get. Very, very imaginative and odd, for the most part.

WWW: What kind of words of wisdom can you give other Web publishing wannabes?
JB: Stop whining, fer chrissakes, and get off your ass and DO it already.

WWW: What kind of person would you like to attract to your site?
JB: Smart and funny people who don't ever, EVER follow the advice given. Ever.

Wander around on the wrong side of the virtual railroad tracks in Cybertown, and you'll find all kinds of strange, bizarre, and twisted Web sites. However, a few manage to stand out. Stroll into Dan's Gallery of the Grotesque and you'll probably get the same feeling I did on first discovering this place ("Dan is a seriously twisted individual"), yet he does have a goal in mind for his disturbing collection:

> *My Gallery of the Grotesque is a metaphor for the squalid, degenerate world that was born out of our own self-indulgence and apathy. Witness here the fabric of our society unravel: We pervert the suffering of others as the fodder for our own debased entertainment, we place those who commit the most deviant acts on pedestals for all to idolize, and we care little about those most in need. The Gallery is a subversive work; it is as offensive as the reality that it exposes. If its iconoclastic contents make you scream out of despair, then your visit was not wasted. If you are convinced that this is simply a collection of disturbing images for your own personal amusement, then you are truly lost.*

http://www.grotesque.com/html/gotg_entrance.html

DAN'S GALLERY OF THE GRO

So disgusting and disturbing are the images in the Gallery that very few of them can be printed. As you stagger through this site, you'll discover a whole collection of photographs of people who met their maker in incredibly violent ways in Necrotica—often with cute descriptions beneath the images:

> *Face Club For Men. This is me, before I discovered the Face Club for Men. That's right, I was an "epidermis-challenged" individual with low self-esteem. I had trouble getting a job, and meeting women—well, let's just say that "Run For Your Lives" was my nickname. But that all changed when a friend of my suggested The Face Club for Men. Now, I have a great career working as a crash test dummy, and the women flock to me like a babe magnet. So call today, before you find your nose in your soup.*

From a hapless individual who somehow got his head caught in a garbage truck's press to some poor soul who decided to do a tightrope walk along a high-tension power line, the images come fast and furious.

From here you can wander into Flatland—kind of like the Squashed Bug Zoo (page 22)—except with humans. Still can't quite envision it? Take an M-1 tank, add one Iraqi soldier in the wrong place at the wrong time, then photograph the result.

Other areas include Gross Misconceptions (the opposite of cute baby pictures), The Petting Zoo (which has pictures of our furry friends in horrible poses), and Ultraviolence (need I say more?).

Two sections of particular interest include America's Least Wanted, which contains images from the headlines that you never saw: Kurt Cobain's autopsy images, John Bobbitt's severed penis, Nicole Brown Simpson's murder scene, and the suicide of R. Budd Dwyer, former Pennsylvania State Treasurer, who called a press conference and then, in front of dozens of video cameras, pulled out a .357 Magnum, stuck it in his mouth and pulled the trigger.

To say the Gallery plays on our more morbid side is a vast understatement.

TESQUE

But wait—I've saved the best for last. In an area called Natural Born Losers, Dan has gathered images of two of the dumbest criminals out there. As Dan relates the tale:

For your consideration:

A biker bimbette decided that she'd rather be rid of her husband, so she coaxed her boyfriend to stop by for an impromptu soiree. As she beguiled her hubby by fellating him while he relaxed on the couch, her boyfriend stealthily wandered behind him and stabbed him in the neck. To celebrate her husband's untimely and expeditious demise, the couple proceeded to "get naked," dismember the body, and capture the festivities with their trusty 110 pocket camera.

However, there now was the minor issue of developing the photos. The couple went to a local discount department store where a "friend" worked; he was more than happy to process the film for them. Unfortunately, the individual who packed the prints into the envelope wasn't one of their buddies. This person saw what the photos portrayed and immediately called the authorities.

Needless to say, the photographs made for a charming display as state's evidence at the couple's trial, and the rest of the tale is a matter of public record. Now they're serving 30-to-life sentences in some hell-hole, though in the infinite wisdom of American justice, they will be up for parole in 2014.

Welcome to the shallow end of the gene pool.

The collection of images in this morbid gallery, combined with the cute descriptions added by Dan, are, strangely enough, almost more humorous than disturbing.

Highway 17 Page of Shame

http://got.net/~egallant/the_road.html

Recent medical studies have proven that driving can have an adverse effect on your health. OK, OK, I know—having a horrible accident doesn't do your body any good at all. But these studies show that the stress of driving in normal traffic is extremely bad for your blood pressure and nervous tension. It could effectively shorten one's life just by being so damned difficult. Living here in the San Francisco Bay area, I'm amazed that people don't have more coronaries.

And probably no single stretch of highway can elevate one's blood pressure higher than a lovely little road that winds, and bends, and mutilates

its way from San Jose, California to Santa Cruz. Over this goat trail passes enough traffic to tie up a typical 8-lane freeway…but it's only 4 lanes at best! The name for this little road from heck…Highway 17.

The creator of the Highway 17 Page of Shame has made a real effort to give us someone to point our collective fingers at. By snapping pictures of whomever he deemed the "Jerque du Jour" and matching them with snappy tirades, he hopes to illuminate the dastardly fiends behind snarled traffic.

What about those rubberneckers who slow down because of the appearance of a tow truck along the road?

"Jeepers, Pa! Is that one of those new-fangled tow-trucks on the side of the road? Let's come to a complete stop so I kin take a gander at it!"

---

interview with **EMIL H. GALLANT**

WWW: What drove you (heh, heh) to create this site?
EG: Dealing with the biggest idiots behind the wheel day in and day out on the worst possible "highway."

WWW: Were there any accomplices?
EG: I started the Page of Shame with Curtis Feigel, my carpool partner.

WWW: What are your goals?
EG: World peace or a better commute.

WWW: Where and how do you gather your content?
EG: I drove to work and got bitter. Really, it was that simple.

WWW: What kind of reaction do people have to this site?
EG: My friends thought it was great—most of them have to drive the same road, so they understood exactly what I was trying to

Or maybe one of those snotty beauty queens (or kings) who seems more absorbed in tweaking their appearance than driving:

So you're cruising down the highway and you glance up in the rearview mirror. Uh oh, you're hair is a complete mess! It's not like you're some vain, conceited marketing dweeb, but really, it's a knotty, tangled mess! Do you wait until you get to the office and brush it out in the parking lot? Hell no—someone could see you and think to themselves, "Look at that slob! Did squirrels nest in that hair?" The smart (and fashionable) thing to do is root around and find your brush, adjust your mirror so you can get a real good look at your head, and start working on making you beautiful again.

On and on the vituperation flows, venting the anger of the ages on dippy drivers. From the idiot who cuts you off WITHOUT USING A TURN SIGNAL—to the giant rock-laden trucks that lumber up the hill IN THE FAST LANE—to smoking wrecks that should never be allowed on the road but always seem to end up RIGHT IN FRONT OF YOU.

Spend a while reading through the Highway 17 Page of Shame, and you'll first find yourself angry at all the numbnuts drivers out there—then sheepishly self-conscious when you read about someone who drives the same car that you do—and finally, enlightened to realize we could all end up on the Highway 17 Page of Shame, because we all sometimes leave our brains in a jar by the bed when we head out the door to drive somewhere.

So the next time you're stuck behind one of those ponderous Cadillacs driven by a little old lady who can barely see over the steering wheel, remember the Highway 17 Page of Shame and the lessons learned—and be happy, because it could be a lot worse. You could be following one of those damned snooty Saab drivers—and we *all* know what a bunch of jerks they are!

do. Some local Highway Patrol guys have seen it and unofficially enjoy it, but they can't officially say they like it, because I get kinda rude and make sweeping generalizations based on the brand of car that people drive.

WWW: Your relatives?
EG: The wired ones thought it was cool and the non-wired ones didn't really understand it until they saw it on CNN. My mom thought it was funny, but told me to watch out for the wackos out there with guns.

WWW: How has the Web-wandering community reacted to it?
EG: The response from the Web has been great! Bitching about other people's driving skills is a worldwide pastime, and people really get off on it.

WWW: Have you learned any lessons from doing something this bizarre?
EG: Not really, except that there are always people out there who are weirder than yourself. Oh yeah, and Catholics don't have a very good sense of humor.

WWW: What advice do you have for other Web publishers?
EG: Stop talking and start writing HTML.

T H E **K O**

M U S E **U**

http://www.teleport.com/~dkossy/

Donna Kossy believes that kooks have gotten a bad rap.

As she writes in the introduction to her book, **Kooks: A Guide to the Outer Limits of Human Belief** *(©1994, Donna Kossy and Feral House):*

> *The word "kook" was coined by beatniks, as a pared-down version of "cuckoo," as in "going cuckoo." A kook is a person stigmatized by virtue of outlandish, extreme or socially unacceptable beliefs that underpin their entire existence. Kooks usually don't keep their beliefs to themselves; they either air them constantly or create lasting monuments to them.*

So it seems appropriate that she created the Kook's Museum in the ideal new medium for kooks, the World Wide Web. She continues her description of the museum:

> *As curator and founder of the first Kook's Museum in history, I am fulfilling a half-lifelong goal of housing kook ideas from all over the world under one crumbling roof. Here, my Solution to the World Problem collection will finally have a home ... Here ancient perpetual motion devices will sit side-by-side with the latest in anti-gravity technology.*

The Kook's Museum is a fascinating place from the moment you log in to the lobby. Right off the bat, I wandered off down the Conspiracy Corridor (I think it was to shake those government agents who were in cahoots with the aliens that moved into the house next door). Here I was able to learn all about the horrible secret hidden in this "New World Order" thing: that John Lennon was actually done in by Stephen King on orders from Richard Nixon—and that Jimmy Carter is actually the biological father of Bill Clinton (have you noticed how similar their voices are?). This particular part of the museum is enough to leave any confident American wondering if there isn't something fishy going on around here.

The Library of Questionable Scholarship houses excerpts from MIT's Archive of Useless Research, among others (no, I didn't find anything relating to the Star Wars defense plan).

The Solution to the World Problem exhibit contains valuable information on the Voluntary Human Extinction Movement ("Thank you for not breeding") along with other interesting solutions to many of our woes.

The Hall of Hate is a wonderful place to take it all out on whatever group you find convenient to blame for your problems; candidates include SCUM (The Society to Cut Up Men). Also present are Whites accusing Blacks, Blacks accusing Whites, and everybody accusing Jews. To put it mildly, this isn't a really NICE place.

The Gallery of the Gods will truly confuse those at odds with their religious beliefs.

And you can rack up plenty of screen time wandering through the Hall of Quackery, to Monuments to Kookdom, to links to other sources of kook-related information all over the Web.

 interview with **DONNA KOSSY**

WWW: What was your inspiration for this site?
DK: Twelve years' worth of inspiration by odd characters who would rather tell the world about their ideas on how to fix everything than sit around watching TV. People who believe stuff that others think is absurd are intriguing to me. I never get tired of wondering what led them to believe what they do.

WWW: Were there any accomplices?
DK: There are always contributors, but I do all the organizing, decision-making, graphics, and editing. People frequently suggest sites to link to, and a couple of people have contributed articles. People frequently tell me about their favorite kook or their latest kook Web discovery.

WWW: What are your goals?
DK: I want people to leave my site saying, "Hmmmmm." I want people to think (about their own beliefs, for example), and I also want them to see the humor in the bizarre world we live in.

WWW: How much effort was this page?
DK: In relation to what? Sometimes I spend hours and hours redesigning something. When I began, a lot of effort went into the planning and design, but the texts were mostly taken from articles I'd already written.

WWW: Where and how do you gather your content?
DK: I've been collecting kook docs for years by mail order and also by chance. I keep my eyes open for weird literature wherever I go. People also know to send their weird literature to me, so a good portion of the material is donated. But then there are always those odd flyers posted on telephone poles.

WWW: What kind of reaction did your friends have to this site?
DK: They know what I do already and knew what to expect more or less. People have generally loved the site. In fact, it's gotten me more media attention than anything else I've ever done.

WWW: The local police?
DK: Ha ha! Actually, several people have been offended by my Hall of Hate. You're not supposed to see any humor in hate any more, I guess. And god forbid you provide access to hate literature itself. I think it's important to have access to all points of view, no matter how odious. And also to poke fun at some of it.

WWW: How has the Web-wandering community reacted to it?
DK: Overwhelmingly positive, as I said, with a couple offended parties here and there. The response has gone beyond my wildest dreams, in fact. I've been linked to by zillions of sites—once, the amount of traffic broke Teleport (my Internet service).

WWW: Have you learned any lessons from doing something this bizarre?
DK: First, not everyone appreciates this stuff, and people are going to peg you as that "weird" person. Once you do something different (like Kook's), people are always going to remember you as the person who did Kook's—they won't let you forget it, and they always want more of the same.

WWW: What words of wisdom can you offer other potential Web publishers?
DK: To me, the "Web" part is irrelevant, though it is much easier to publish on the Web than elsewhere. But anyway, all I can say is don't be afraid to fool around and have fun with it. That's what it's there for.

bianca's Smut shack

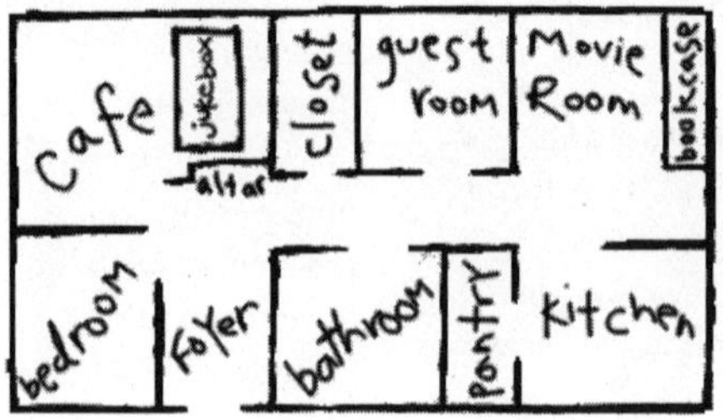
cafe
jukebox
altar
closet
guest room
Movie Room
bookcase
bedroom
foyer
bathroom
pantry
kitchen

http://shack.bianca.com/shack/index.html

The only real problem with wandering the weird side of the Web is that some of the more memorable sites are anything but permanent. Find the be-all end-all twisted salute to O.J. Simpson's knife collection this week, and by the time your friends try to check it out, it's moved or vanished into cyberspace.

A few sites, though, develop longevity. One of the most *unusual* of these is bianca's Smut Shack. bianca has been serving up smut for over two years. The Shack has become less a site and more a community wherein you can wander, read, and then scrawl your own graffiti—that is, if you're over 18.

Using a floor plan to navigate, you can start your adventure in bianca's Bathroom, where you'll find three stalls: the communal stall, the graffiti stall, and the dumping stall. You can chat, add your wisdom to the walls, or carry on a spirited conversation about the Daily Dump. As bianca's soothing voice urges:

> So, please remove yourself from the pressures of the real world, and discuss your dump. Relax, no one has to know it's you. Come, come, share with the world, we all secretly want to know how you do it.

Wander over to the Bedroom, and you can check out bianca's sacred diary, her strange and bizarre dreams, or her vast collection of sex toys. Yes, the word "smut" is appropriate in many parts of the site. There's a chat going on here as well. To say that it's appropriate for the bedroom is putting it mildly.

Her Kitchen is filled with all sorts of stuff, including a cookbook of recipes that are seriously twisted—including one that involves filling a turkey with popcorn kernels, tying it tight, placing it in a 400-degree oven, and waiting until the laws of physics have their way.

The Pantry is filled with all sorts of junk, including bianca's collection of stuff made from duct tape:

> Next to her own juices, duct tape is bianca's favorite substance in the world! Oh, so many uses it has! To date, bianca hasn't found a problem her duct tape couldn't fix. People know they can come to bianca for any sort of duct tape needed. And though bianca likes to keep her duct tape in the pantry, she always takes it with her whenever she leaves the shack. One never knows where duct tape will come in handy.

As is the case all over this site, bianca also wants your suggestions for new uses of the tape that holds the universe together, such as:

> Holding your ears down while riding in your convertible.

> Taping carpet samples to my feet, so no matter where I go, it's always carpeted!!

> I use duck tape to tape two ducks together. Although it really quacks me up, it's always a pair o' ducks as to what to do next!

The rest of the rooms include a Guest Room, a Movie Room (she's always looking for submissions), and the Coffee Shop. Is bianca's Smut Shack for everyone? Well, not necessarily…but it's still a hell of a lot of fun.

RELIGION
religion

The Mother of All Holy Wars

It was bound to happen some day: Get enough religions together, and you'll eventually find conflicts arising with disasterous results. Such is the case when the Church of the Gerbil and the Church of the Bunny began to share the same cyberspace.

Trumpeting Elmer Fudd's famous words "Kill the wabbit!" the Church of the Gerbil proclaimed, "Go Forth And Bring All Other Small Furry Mammalian Religions Under The Umbrella Of The Gerbil King, For Only There Can We Live In Harmony," and thus fired the first volley of the ensuing conflict. The Church of the Bunny was quick to respond with a formal statement denouncing this proclamation. By then announcing that the Bunny was actually a Pig in disguise, the Church of the Gerbil upped the ante—with attitude.

Where will all of this lead? Will sites on the World Wide Web fall prey to religious terrorism? Will the Internet become the next Northern Ireland or Gaza Strip? Only time will tell. But for now, the fur is literally flying.

CHURCH OF THE MIGHTY GERBIL

http://pages.prodigy.com/gerbilism.html/

People on the World Wide Web appear to be always on the lookout for unusual religious icons. Take Mc Church's McDonna, or the Intergalactic House of Fruitcakes—or the Church of the Gerbil.

Gerbil?

Yes, those wonderfully cute little rodents have spawned their own religion, and it's got the members of the Church of the Bunny hopping mad! (Sorry, but I couldn't miss one that easy.)

The church got its start, at least according to its own literature, when Hacim (pronounced hakeem) was visited by a messanger from god, a chinchilla, who told him, "You have been chosen to spread the word of the great benevolent (though sometimes evil) members of the holy family *Gerbillus*."

Soon afterwords the Church of the Gerbil was started. The church is built on several basic premises:

> 1. God is a Gerbil. This is a proven fact. Why else would there be Zippy the Pinhead, butterflies, rainbows, hamsters, and flowers?

(continued on page 134, GERBIL)

THE CHURCH OF THE BUNNY

http://ourworld.compuserve.com:80 /homepages/bunnychurch/

Many of the churches found in cyberspace are relatively young, especially when you compare them with more established religious organizations. Of course that makes sense, because there were no computers in the times of Moses, or Jesus, or even Bud Willis (he founded the little-known Church of Bud in his hometown in the hills of Arkansas. He got only his cousin Dave to join, and even he quit as soon as he sobered up...but I digress).

But there are some churches online that are at least a little bit older than others. One of the oldest, The Church of the Bunny, got its start in a CompuServe chat area in 1990. Pope Rich tells of the origins of the church, when he began to deface a religious comic book he'd received by adding a pair of bunny ears to a portrait of God.

> *At first, I just laughed it off as a weird little picture, but in time I came to realize that there was a definite reason that the picture had shown a Bunny. It was a sign from the Being that would become my deity, and around whom I would form a new religion. It was a direct sign from The*

(continued on page 135, BUNNY)

(GERBIL, continued from page 133)

2. The Supreme Gerbil fashioned the universe after a treadmill. It created all fuzzy creatures from its ideals of beauty. It created humans to take care of the fuzzy ones (to clean, cook, and take out the dirty newspapers) so that the fuzzy creatures would be free from worldly troubles.

3. Since God is a Gerbil, microwaves are hell, and Richard Gere is the devil.

4. If you bury a Gerbil (in the prescribed manner described in The Book of Gerbil), it will rise again in three days.

5. Gerbils are the superior beings.

6. Gerbils always look on the bright side of life.

7. Evil Gerbils are often reincarnated as one of the more base life forms, most horribly, humans.

The Church of Gerbil hasn't grown very big yet; Though, it's got quite a bit of competition from other "lesser religions" like the Catholics and Muslims. But its symbol is a lot cuter so it does have potential there.

When I stumbled onto the Church of the Gerbil, I was a bit disturbed. When I was a young boy, my parents gave me several gerbils, with which I had many hours of fun. Unfortunately, our cat became jealous and wanted to play with the furry friends herself, so late one night, she got their cage open and had fun with rodents—and she also had quite a tasty meal. What really disturbed me was that if this church does prove that God is a Gerbil, my family's cat ate God.

Hmmm—it kind of makes you wonder about things, doesn't it?

Or maybe not.

interview with ST. REVEREND TONY JORDAN

WWW: What was your inspiration for this site?
SRTJ: The Church of the Gerbil is primarily an offline phenomenon. Hacim is a real person named Micah Olguin, who came up with the idea of Gerbilism. I helped conceptualize it and have expanded it, but he is the true messiah.

WWW: Were there any accomplices?
SRTJ: All those named on the page of saints. Primarily, the twelve opposums had some influence on the church. I myself, however, created the Web page.

WWW: What are your goals?
SRTJ: My goal is to spread the loving word of the Gerbil to all corners of the universe, to buy a computer for college, to asimilate the Church

of the Bunny, and to get Yahoo! to put my page in a better category.

WWW: How much effort was this page?
SRTJ: As most soul-searching works are, it was taxing both physically and emotionally. After making the page, I went into a three-week coma.

WWW: Where and how do you gather your content?
SRTJ: My content comes from the Gerbil itself, it is not gathered, but rather given.

WWW: What kind of reaction did your friends have to this site?
SRTJ: They love it. Most often, people renounce their current religion and send me lots of money. I hope that new visitors keep this up.

(continue on page 136, GERBIL)

church of the mighty gerbil

(BUNNY, continued from page 133)

Bunny Himself!! As time went on, I was enlightened by more of The Bunny's Ways. He came to me in a dream and told me of the Flaming Pit of Jello, which is purported to be in Wheeling, West Virginia, and is the place of eternal damnation for those who would seek to destroy The Bunny. He told me to go out into the world, for others had insight into His Ways, and together, we would form the big fuzzy jigsaw puzzle that is the Church of the Bunny.

One interesting thing about the Church of the Bunny is that, believe it or not, it IS a real church with members all over the world. Not exactly thousands, but dozens ain't bad. Their basic creed is one of tolerance. The majority of the site focuses on profiles of the various leaders of the church, except for announcements of a potential holy war brewing. As Pope Rich puts it,

> Bunnies and Bun-Seekers, please be warned! We have an adversary right hare on the Web! The Church of the Gerbil has declared a Holy War on us. Apparently, Cyberspace ain't big enough for two religions who worship cute, fuzzy little creatures. We hare at the CoB are a peace-loving group, but if you know anything about Bunnies, you know how nasty we can be when we are threatened! (BIG, pointy teeth, and all that.) Personally, I think that Saint Tony and his followers will eventually see the Bun-Light, and peace will ooze from every orifice of the Net.

> But we'll have to see, won't we?

It's apparent that things are heating up on the more spiritual side of the Net.

interview with **POPE RICH**

WWW: What was your inspiration or, more accurately, what drove you to create this site?

PR: My inspiration for creating this Web site was simple: to spread the Joy of the Bunny to the rest of the world and beyond. Up until recently, we'd been restricted to our hutch in CompuServe's Religion Forum. But with the surge in the popularity of the Web, we saw an excellent opportunity to reach out to the other truly strange and tweaked minds on the planet.

WWW: Were there any accomplices, or are you the only one that can be held liable?

PR: My accomplices are several, many of whom are linked to my site. Chief among them would be my Elders— Executive Vice-Pope TJ, Vice-Pope Doug, Archbunhop (now Cardinal) Cyn, Wise Man Dan, and many others. Doug and Dan were probably the first to suggest expanding to the Web, and as soon as the technology became cheap and easy (that is, CompuServe offered it as part of membership), we jumped right in!

WWW: What are your long-term goals?

PR: My goal is simple: world domination! Hahahahahaaaa! Just kidding. Spreading the Joy of the Bunny, I guess. The majority of the world's religions take themselves far too seriously, to the point that religious differences have become one of the most divisive forces in society today. The CoB looks to change that. We offer an alternative where people can put aside their differences

(continue on page 136, BUNNY)

the church of the bunny

135

(GERBIL, continued from page 134)

WWW: The local police?
SRTJ: They, too, fully support the Gerbil King.

WWW: How has the Web-wandering community reacted to it?
SRTJ: Usually very favorably. Two or three people are setting up their own online and offline churches (which are always welcome) and, except for a few ignorant souls, most people really like it. Besides if you don't like it, you'll go to hell.

WWW: How do you feel now that it's up?
SRTJ: I like it—however, it will be revised and updated at the Gerbil's request.

WWW: What's next?
SRTJ: The war with the Bunny will be accented, as well as the branch religions and other top-secret things. Prepare to be shocked.

WWW: Have you learned any lessons from doing something this bizarre?
SRTJ: I normally don't learn from mistakes.

WWW: What words of wisdom can you offer potential Web publishers?
SRTJ: If you need weird guidance—pray.

The Church of the Bunny

SANCTUS TEMPLUM ET CUNICULUS

(BUNNY, continued from page 135)

and accentuate their similarities. Basically, we're saying that Our Myth's as good as Your Myth, so let's cut the crap, and have some fun! (paraphrased from a quote by Saint Bill Potts, CoB)

WWW: How much effort did it take to create this page?
PR: Putting together the site was not too much effort, thanks mostly to CompuServe's HomePage Wizard software. It was easy, but real limited as far as its flexibility. So I hope to redo the whole thing with more advanced HTML software. That will probably take a little

more effort—such as learning HTML commands, and so on.

WWW: Where and how did you gather your content?
PR: Content was pretty straightforward. A little about the church, a little about myself, that sort of stuff. Then I just linked the other CoB members and some sites that I liked. Picked up a few URLs from Yahoo! for stuff that caught my eye. Then, as time went by, people would check out my page and e-mail me with stuff that was appropriate, and I'd add a link to some of those. It's very audience-

church of the mighty gerbil

participation-ish, really.

WWW: How did your friends react to your site when you first told them about it? Your family? The police?
PR: Friends' reactions have varied. Several of my friends already knew about the CoB, and some were members. Other people had a variety of reactions, from hysterical delight to total confusion (either one of which is pretty cool). Relatives, same sort of thing. My brothers love it. My parents are pretty religious, so I haven't mentioned it to them. My mother was sort of displeased when she found out my e-mail address, so I didn't feel that it was a good time to suggest they check out my Web page. The local police, at this point, have not mentioned it to me. But I'm sure they're laughing so hard that they're spewing donut crumbs all over their monitors! (I speak facetiously. I have nothing but the utmost respect for local law enforcement. Please don't ticket my car!)

WWW: How has the Web-wandering community reacted to it?
PR: Reaction from the Web wanderers has been pretty good. I've only had one complaint, about how it's sort of sacrilegious or something, and that was very pleasantly worded. Apart from that, I've had nothing but good comments flooding my mailbox. And I've made quite a few new friends.

WWW: How do you feel now that your site is up?
PR: I'm pretty happy about the Web page. I do plan to update it in the near future with a better HTML setup, so it's a little more streamlined. But it's pretty cool, and the people seem to like it.

WWW: What's next?
PR: What's next? I'm not sure. A little over two years ago, this church was nothing more than an inside joke among a few people. I never imagined at that point that it would take off like this. So whatever happens next, just happens. It's in the paws of the Bunny. I defer to His control.

WWW: Have you learned any lessons from doing something this bizarre?
PR: I've learned a few things from doing this. If I may quote Robert Downey, Jr., in "Air America": "Where I come from, I'm used to being the weirdest guy in the room. Out here, I'm not even in the running!" In other words, there are a lot of really tweaked people out there, and I'm happy as hell to get a chance to interact with them. On a deeper, more serious level, The Church of the Bunny has opened my eyes to a lot of things. I've become a lot more open to different lifestyles and viewpoints, and in turn, become more tolerant of other people. Interacting with some of the people I've encountered online, both through the Web page and otherwise, has helped me see life in a different way. Believe it or not, I am actually more at peace with myself than I ever was before. But I'm rambling, aren't I?

WWW: What words of wisdom would you give other lost souls who have this itch they just gotta scratch to put up a truly weird Web wonder?
PR: Go for it! If there's something you have to say, or something you want to do, get your sorry butt on the Web and let everyone know! You'll be amazed at the response!

WWW: What kind of person would you like to attract to a site like this?
PR: Everyone, really. Most ideally, anyone with a slightly off-center view of the world and an open mind. I don't even mind if people don't like my site. Some people won't. But a lot of people do. And those are my kind of people.

THE INTERGALACTIC HOUSE OF FRUITCAKES

The InterGalactic House of Fruitcake doesn't spend time lecturing you on its merits when you arrive; it immediately launches a musical chorus singing praise. The screen then reads:

> *Welcome to the InterGalactic House of Fruitcake's home page, the authoritative Web site of all things OTISian, and the only fully registered Web site for the Last True Faith on this pathetic little planet.*

Little doubt is left about the attitude found here. This site also differentiates itself from other "religious" sites by the heavy graphics on their home page and its sparse text. No long treatises, no deep proclamations.

When you click on "Handy Hints for the Unwashed Heathen," you'll find a quick guide to "The Last TRUE FAITH on this Pathetic Little PLANET."

Delve even further to find out just what the heck OTIS is, and you'll find that OTIS isn't some bored grad student in Switzerland or a sysop in New Jersey on the late shift—it really is a god—or so it seems...

OTIS is the main god/dess we worship. (S)he is at the head of our pantheon. OTIS is an ancient god/dess of life. His/her worship started about 2,000 years before Christ, making him/her one of the oldest god(desse)s in existence. OTIS worship originated in ancient Sumeria, survived in cult form in the Roman empire, and was squashed by the Christians during the "witch hunts" of the 15th century. It remained that way until we resurrected it (with our own peculiar modifications) during the 1980s. As you may have already guessed, OTIS is neither male nor female. His/her symbol is four arrows going in opposite directions with the top arrow separate and the other three joined. No one is sure what this means.

Frankly, Tim and I made it up because it looked nice. OTIS is the god/dess of life.

Continue and you eventually find the dogma of this religion. Gosh, these Internet-based churches are so EASY!

We have no dogma, you should have known. Shame, shame.

Everything forbidden is optional; 'Do what we would not have thou do' shall be the whole of the law.

Send us money!

You'll also discover that these people aren't happy with one god; they've got a whole passel of 'em, including Lotus (a Taiwanese god), Rhotus (the god of death they made up), and Spode (a Celtic god). In addition, there are also four bad gods: Blix, Grbl, Vootie, and Wayne (the deities of Pain, Suffering, Disease, and New Jersey, respectively) and the Anti-OTIS, the notorious 'B. OTIS, Too' (terribly evil god and remarkably snappy dresser).

Finally, there are literally dozens of miscellaneous entities including God X (The God of Comparative Shopping) and Mari-Lyn (Goddess of Sex and Eliminatory Functions). You begin to get the idea that this could be a pretty complicated religion.

 interview with **JEFF STEVENS**

WWW: What was your inspiration for this site?
JS: Well, the religion (OTISianism) came first, and the Web pages followed. I publish to promote OTISianism. I promote OTISianism because a very Large and Impressive God/dess told me I had better.

OTISians have been on the Internet longer than any other "fringe" faith, save the Erisians (who have been out here so long they're growing mold). We started with The Purple Thunderbolt of Spode ("Purps" for short). I had been putting out a number of snail mail/paper publications, including our weekly mailings and the really rather infamous *OTISian Directory*. At college I suddenly had access to the Bitnet, and it didn't take long to realize that here was a chance to publish cheaply (OTIS is virtu-

ally FREE, thanks to Uncle Sam). So I made the move from the marginals to the margins of the Internet. I was shocked to discover that the potential market on the Net for The Last TRUE FAITH on this Pathetic Little Planet was enormous. Purps went from twenty subscribers to over a hundred within months, and continued to grow at an astonishing clip (you'd have to ask Mal3, the current editor, how many people read it now, but I think we're somewhere between the subscription rates for *Ferret Legging News* and *Time*).

When the Web emerged, I had my very own (Steve) Jobsian revelation that it would completely reconfigure the Internet and change forever the way in which we interacted with it. And, OTIS, it was *still cheap*. What more motivation would any serious Pope need? By this time OTISianism had been around so long and inspired so many others to produce OTISian dogma, myths, and legends (not to mention heresies, sects, and false prophecies) that I had no trouble finding material. OTIS

None of it had any structure of course, but the wonderful thing about the Web is that it requires no structure. I taught myself HTML in a weekend (by looking at the source of other people's pages) and had a site up and running four days later (Hail OTIS!).

JS: Like all good shows, the IGHF pages are made possible by a cast of thousands. I mentioned Mal3 (who, in addition to Purps, has given us a gopher and anonymous FTP site), and he deserves a great deal of credit. Without his hard work the FBI wouldn't NEED a full time crew watching my house (Hail Spode). Other notables include Archbishop Chad Hessoun, OTISOTIS Scott "Doc" Simpson, and Preacher Tim Howland.

The moral: Web pages are like sex. You can go it alone, but the involvement of other people is preferable.

WWW: What are your goals?
JS: Complete world domination in the name of OTIS. To CRUSH the infidels under the mighty boot of OTISian progress. To spread the truths of OTISianism to the four corners of the globe. To make the Last True Faith the major faith on this pathetic little planet.

I also want one of those bubble cars like the other Pope has. It's nifty.

WWW: How much effort was creating this page?
JS: I spent endless days and nights cranking out just the first few lines of code. I never slept. I barely ate. My dog didn't recognize me anymore. My wife threatened me with divorce (not our divorce, mind you, someone else's; but I still couldn't help feeling that something was wrong). I kept thinking there had to be a better way. And then one night it hit me: child labor. The very next morning I began importing orphans from Canada and having them write code for $0.18 per hour. I heartily recommend child labor to anyone seriously considering Web publishing. :)

WWW: Where and how do you gather your content?
JS: The OTISian dogma, of course, has existed for countless millennia; some of it is even older than Atlantis. It existed in huge dusty boxes in my basement, just daring me to find a good use for it. The art I stole from friends while they weren't paying attention. So I was lucky to have ready-made content close at hand. Still, one of the most over commented-upon aspects of the Web is the frighteningly low standard of what constitutes Web content. People believe that everything interesting has already been said and resort to submitting a copy of the Pope's laundry list. Which is where all those uninteresting sites that offer nothing but reviews of other, even less-interesting sites come from. There's a lesson in here for aspiring publishers, incidentally, but I'm not going to tell you what it is just yet. I'm saving it for a future series of Web pages. Oh, and by the bye, I've already done the laundry-list thing, too

(http://challenge.tiac.
net/users/ighf/laundry
.html). Get your own
idea.

**WWW: What kind of re-
action did your friends
have to this site?**
JS: As faithful
OTISians they were
overjoyed to see that
the Last True Faith on
this pathetic little
planet was being
spread to the masses
via a new and exciting
medium. This is ab-
solutely true. Pay no
attention to what they
tell you.

WWW: Your relatives?
JS: As faithful
OTISians they were
overjoyed to see that
the Last True Faith on
this pathetic little
planet was being
spread to the masses
via a new and exciting
medium. This is ab-
solutely true. Pay no
attention to what they
tell you.

WWW: The local police?
JS: Were bought off
long ago.

**WWW: How has the
Web-wandering com-
munity reacted to it?**
JS: At first with the
studied apathy and
indifference the
denizens of the Web
are famous for. But
slowly the Web has
warmed to us, and we
to it. It turns out the
Web is a natural home
for this kind of satiric
silliness; at the mo-
ment a search for IGHF
on your favorite search
engine (mine's Alta
Vista, get your own)
will yield SEVEN PAGES
of links. If you build
it, they will come.
Granted, the neighbors
will still think you're
nuts.

**WWW: How do you feel
now that it's up?**
JS: Genki!

WWW: What's next?
JS: World conquest.
Oh, you mean the
pages? A greatly ex-
panded Leo A. Yuspeh
Archives section for a
startOTIS. More multi-
media, of course.
Despite the rumors, a
six-hour Quicktime
presentation of the

Pope walking up and
down stairs is not in
the works, but I'm
working on video-
taping some of the
more popular OTISian
ceremonies and adding
a number of sound
bites. And of course
the revised, updated
version of the Pope's
laundry list.

**WWW: Have you
learned any lessons
from doing something
this bizarre?**
JS: This isn't bizarre.
You're talking to a guy
who OTISOTIS hosted a
radio talk show naked
as a way of boosting
ratings, OTISOTIS tried
to get the "rod,"
"cubit," and "league"
reinstated as national
measurements, and
attempted to place a
motion before
Congress to have
North Dakota and
Vermont secede from
the United States
(Vermont because it
was thinking about it
already and North
Dakota because no
one's really using it
anyway. Hail Spode!).

Those are *bizarre*. The
pages are really quite
sane.

**WWW: Any words of
wisdom for other lost
souls who want to
create a Web page?**
JS: OTIS, this is the
kind of question I
hate—the kind that
demands a serious
answer. I still think
everyone should have
their own Web
page.*OTIS*

Grab a piece of the
8Clectric wilderness
before it's paved over
for a virtual parking
lot and DO SOMETHING
BETTER with the space
than what Microsoft
and Walt Disney have
planned. The strange,
the wild, the weird,
and the bizarre will
never be the majority
for long. But we can
claim a piece for our-
selves. Web pages are
easy and cheap. Throw
one up for yourself
before Mitsubishi does
one for you.

**WWW: What kind of
person would you like
to attract to a site like
this?**
JS: Gullible and rich.
And anyone slightly
(or maybe more than
slightly) at odds with
consensus reality. As
the Cacophonies say,
you may already be a
member. Welcome, and
Hail OTIS!

"Absurdistan is a lovely country somewhere between the North and South Pole," begins the Absurdistan Web site. It goes on to reveal that in Absurdistan it rains 365 days a year, sometimes 366. The Absurdistan page isn't really like any other travel page on the Web. It isn't filled with sunny pictures of sunny people having sunny fun—I mean, it rains EVERY DAY OF THE YEAR.

Fortunately for great world travelers, the page includes a list of important tips on traveling in Absurdistan:

If you get lost use the map. If you don't know how to use a map, get lost.

Have your blood pressure checked every 15 minutes.

Put your wallet under the keyboard.

If some statement doesn't make sense to you, try multiplying it by 2+3i.

Don't talk to the computer screen in the presence of your supervisor.

New links are either red or yellow. The used ones are blue or pink, depending on the background. Don't follow links with strange colors or smells.

If you are attacked by birds, press the F1 key. If your keyboard doesn't have it, smash the birds with a mouse. For best results use the "first come, first served" principle.

The standard voltage in Absurdistan is 99V. Please adjust your coffee maker.

Avoid lions. They are NOT user friendly.

For transportation use Netscape (strongly recommended), Mosaic, or Cimrman's Webus.

If you don't understand something, don't worry. The chances are that I don't get it either.

Absurdistan is a rather unusual country. Its land area is occupied by 28.8% city dumps, its chief exports are coal, iron ore, and tooth brushes; its population varies with the seasons; its agricultural industry includes strawberries, weasel farms, and happy cows (who are probably happy because lots of hungry tigers occupy the countries surrounding Absurdistan but can't get in). Even though it has several political parties, it is under the dictatorship of a president who is in absentia (which may be somewhere north of Absurdistan).

http://www.trail.com/~honza

The government is described as follows:

Form: The Absurd Party is in full control of the capital. All the bills proposed by it are automatically passed. The Senate convenes only on Saturdays as a marching band for a football team. Away from Ejsi the form of government is looser and, close to the border, it approaches anarchy.

Ejsi, D.C., the capital of Absurdistan, claims to have the largest underground airport in the world, which is unfortunate, because no airlines will land there. It is also home to a newspaper with the largest circulation in the world, but unfortunately, the local residents don't know where there are any newsstands—so nobody has actually ever seen it. Ejsi also appears to be a rather paranoid place:

Ejsi is so secret that if you ask for the map of Ejsi anywhere in Absurdistan, you'll get a blank sheet of paper. That way the Party makes sure that nobody can deduce where all its "goodies" are. Some say (jokingly) that the Ejsi city map is the world's most published city map because any time a clean sheet of paper is produced in a paper mill, one more Ejsi city map is effectively printed. And that's a lot.

Ejsi is a paradise for schoolkids. In any subject, "That's a secret" is considered to be the only right answer. Of course, given these circumstances, the kids in Absurdistan have the highest grade point average in the world.

Delve further through this site and you'll find one of the great sources of national pride—well, not really. In fact, most local residents are thoroughly disgusted by Pink Mountain, revealed here in high resolution black and white. Hmm…it almost looks like—nah, it can't be.

So, the next time you need to get away from it all, consider lovely Absurdistan. Now if only I could find it on a world map.

interview with **JAN REHACEK**

WWW: What was your inspiration for this site?
JR: Peer pressure. I noticed that most of my friends already had their own pages, so I thought I'd have one too. I was disappointed at the common format of a photo with links, so I decided to actually write something on it.

WWW: What are your goals?
JR: Become a professional mathematician.

WWW: How much effort was this page?
JR: Not much. I wrote the basic stuff during the summer of '95 and since then I write something here and there, as I have time.

WWW: Where and how do you go about gathering your content?
JR: I downloaded the icons and stuff from other Web sites, and the writing is original. I just write when something occurs to me.

WWW: What kind of reaction did your friends and family have to this site?
JR: My friends liked it; my relatives haven't seen it yet.

WWW: The local police?
JR: There is no local police in Absurdistan. APD is global.

WWW: How has the Web-wandering community reacted to it?
JR: Absurdistan is just a sketch so far, so I haven't advertised it too much yet—hence I didn't get much reaction (no threats yet, either).

WWW: How do you feel now that it's up?
JR: I feel okay. Blood pressure seems to be quite normal.

WWW: What's next?
JR: I'll expand it a little when I have time and then I'll promote it a bit, so more people know about it.

WWW: Any words of wisdom for other Web publishers?
JR: "The future belongs to aluminium" (Jara Cimrman).

Welcome to
Mc Church® Tabernacle
Home Page

http://mcchurch.org

The Internet is filled with low-budget religions. After spending a day researching the "holy" section of this book, I began to think that anyone with an ego and a little time to kill could start their own church with a minimum of fuss and muss. Yet among this sorry collection of deities, some stood out as serious works. One of the most impressive was the following:

Mc Church starts out by explaining that secret government research had yielded a picture of God that is—well, unflattering:

The report recommended that, "if "God" was an actual member of our society, He should be prevented from contact with impressionable children. Based on the information provided, the analysis clearly showed that "God" would be the type of personality who would be likely to peer at the children entrusted to His care from the dark side of a one-way mirror, occasionally sending cryptic messages to individual children, expecting them to figure it out for themselves or face dire consequences.

The result: It was decided that a new religion should be founded built on a more functional and convenient foundation—Mc Church.

Mc Church is a REAL religion, complete with iconographic images suitable for worship, a martyred saint, snappy advertising slogans, and easy-to-understand spiritual truths that make McWorship as easy as picking up a burger and fries on the way home from work!

Continue on through this site, and you'll witness the age-old debate of Creationism and Evolution given new life using an old technology in the Christian Puppet Theatre. Here our old friends Punch and Judy wail on each other (with a violence befitting the modern tone of this religion) while holding a deep discussion of entropy, calculus, physics, and creationism.

Of course, no religion is fair without having a female image available. Mc Church has McDonna:

The Holy McDonna is the embodiment of womanhood in all aspects, the feminine pathway to your every need: the caring, fiercely protective mother, the tomboy best friend. She is the willing Red Bride who never says "No." Friends, she is a sassy little genie in a bottle ready to help you with your every desperate need or peevish desire.

You can also learn more about the Rev. Dr. O. L. Jaggers and the Rev. Dr. Ma Jaggers, two sources of inspiration, and learn the tragic tale of the McMartyr, once the Prodigal Son, now banished to the farthest corner of the Earth (Thailand, I think?!).

So, does your religion confuse you? Your God frighten the kids? Your Messiah missing? Well, then point your Web browser to the latest, greatest thing in church—Mc Church. And who knows where this faith will ultimately wander? Maybe someday they will find their own messiah. Except, if he is in keeping with the church's philosophy, he'll have bright red hair, big floppy shoes, and a rubber nose that beeps when you squeeze it.

The Holy McDonna

WWW: What was your inspiration for this site?

EP: A friend of mine, Harvey Glunkman, made a seemingly simple request of another friend, McPope: He asked that the spiritually resonant name "Mc Church" be registered as a domain on the Internet for him. At the time, we thought this was a strange thing to ask because Mr. Glunkman did not own a computer.

It turned out that this was to be his last request. A few days later, he performed an act of auto-assumption into Heaven and left us behind. We came to realize that Mr. Glunkman was no ordinary person; in fact, he was the Son of God.

All his life, he had been training us to carry his message to the world. The estab-lishment of the World Wide Web provided the perfect vehicle. With His teaching complete and a suitable tech-nology to achieve his mission established, he left us his final in-structions and passed on. The First Internet Mc Church Tabernacle is a permanent and lasting tribute to his memory.

WWW: Who else was involved in building this site?

EP: That Tabernacle was designed by the original four disciples of Glunkman: myself, McPope, Elder Euka-ryot, and Brother Fred. When the early version of the Tabernacle was unveiled to the world, Sister (Elder) Rosebrit heard the calling and joined us, adding an important doctrinal el-ement to our message.

WWW: Where and how do you gather your content?

EP: We assembled our memories of what our

friend had taught us and realized that he had presented us with a complete doctrinal vision. Each of us had only a part, so until we all got together to compare notes, we didn't realize the significance of what he had left us.

WWW: What kind of reaction did your friends have to this site?
EP: Most of our friends are now McChurch members. Simply by visiting the site and gazing upon the image of the McMartyr, one is *permanently* and *irrevocably* redeemed. This has made us quite popular with the young set. Older people who have spent their life trying to conform to an unachievable set of religious rules are a bit slower to embrace our message; I guess they resist the realization that they have wasted all that effort.

WWW: Your relatives?
EP: The mother of the McMartyr is still alive, but I don't think she has ever seen a computer.

WWW: How has the Web-wandering community reacted to it?
EP: We have been praised and pummeled. Currently in alt.fan.gene-scott, McChurch members are being cruelly persecuted. But most people embrace our teachings and find solace in the fact that once they are redeemed, it can never be taken away from them no matter what they do or what anyone else does. We have found support from Brother Randall of Snake Oil (http:// fender.onramp.net/~a nalyst/snake/Snakeoil .html) and the Rev. Jess of SuperChurch (http://clarksville.mc. utexas.edu/~jess/ superchurch.html).

WWW: What's next?
EP: We are currently creating a "Before

Need" McMortuary Service. The visitor will be able to register their loved ones and see their names inscribed on an appropriate funerary monument. The thing that sets our service aside from those provided by a traditional cemetery is that the loved one need not be dead. Anyone may be enshrined in the McCrypts. This should be very popular.

WWW: Have you learned any lessons from doing something this bizarre?
EP: That there are many paths to the divine. Some paths are steep and difficult to follow; others are twisty and turny with lots of switchbacks and blind alleys. McChurch is the only ten-lane superhighway straight to Heaven. No off-ramps, no speed limits, no toll booths. Just a straight shot to Paradise!

Many religions warn their followers not to

fall in league with people of different faiths, but at McChurch, we encourage everyone to check out the competition. We're confident they'll come back to our simple path again.

WWW: What advice do you have for others who want to publish on the Web?
EP: To quote Mark Twain: "We are all ignorant—just on different subjects." I strongly feel that our ignorance is one of our most endearing traits.

Prayers and supplications may be answered promptly when directed to PermPoom@ McChurch.org.

HANK DUDERSTADT *is an online con-*
sultant, teacher, and journalist whose
articles have appeared in such maga-
zines as Mondo 2000, Morph's
Outpost, *and* Electronic Entertainment.
He lives in Oakland, CA.